on common ground

The Power of
Professional Learning Communities

Solution Tree
formerly national educational service

Copyright © 2005 by Solution Tree
(formerly National Educational Service)
304 West Kirkwood Avenue
Bloomington, Indiana 47404-5132
(812) 336-7700
(800) 733-6786 (toll free)
FAX: (812) 336-7790
e-mail: info@solution-tree.com
www.solution-tree.com

Cover design by Grannan Graphic Design, Ltd.
Text design by T.G. Design Group

Printed in the United States of America

ISBN: 1-932127-42-9

Dedication

We discovered our first sense of "community" as children within our families. Our brothers and sisters were among the first to teach us that individuals with very unique personalities and markedly differing perspectives can find common ground that binds them together through triumphs and trials. Through all the years they have remained our best friends and the people we most admire. We dedicate this book to them.

Russell Burnette
William DuFour
Dana Goetz
Susan Jennings
Denise Kimes
Valerie Robinson

—Rick and Becky DuFour

ᓀ   ᓀ   ᓀ   ᓀ

To my dear friends and co-authors Rick and Becky DuFour whose talent, professionalism, warmth, friendship, and generous spirit never cease to amaze and inspire me.

—Bob Eaker

Table of Contents

About the Editors

Richard DuFour, Robert Eaker, and Rebecca DuFour

Richard DuFour, Ed.D., was a public school educator for 34 years. During his 19-year tenure at Adlai Stevenson High School in Lincolnshire, Stevenson became what the United States Department of Education has described as "one of the most recognized and celebrated schools in America." It is one of only three schools in the nation to win the United States Department of Education (USDE) Blue Ribbon Award on four occasions and has been repeatedly cited in professional literature as an exemplar of best practices in education.

Rick is the author of 7 books and over 40 professional articles. He wrote a quarterly column for the *Journal of Staff Development* for almost a decade. He was the lead consultant and author for the Association of School Curriculum and Development's seven-part video series on the principalship and the author of two other videos: *How to Develop a Professional Learning Community* and *Through New Eyes: Examining the*

Culture of Your School. He was presented the distinguished scholar practitioner award from the University of Illinois and the Distinguished Service Award from the National Staff Development Council. Rick has consulted with school districts, state departments, and professional organizations throughout North America on strategies for improving schools.

Robert Eaker, Ed.D., is the former interim executive vice-president and provost at Middle Tennessee State University, where he also served as dean of the College of Education for 13 years. Bob has written widely on the issues of effective teaching, effective schools, helping teachers use research findings, and high expectations and student achievement. He is co-author of *Creating the New American School* (1992), *Professional Learning Communities at Work* (1998), *Getting Started: Reculturing Schools to Become Professional Learning Communities* (2002), and *Whatever It Takes: How Professional Learning Communities Respond When Kids Don't Learn* (2004). He has spoken at numerous national meetings, such as the National Association of Secondary School Principals and the Association for Supervision and Curriculum Development, and he was chosen by Phi Delta Kappa for the "People in Educational Evaluation and Research" interview series that appeared in the October 1986 issue of *Phi Delta Kappan.* In 2003 the Student Government Association of Middle Tennessee State University recognized Bob with the Distinguished Faculty Award. Bob regularly consults with school districts throughout North America on school improvement issues.

Rebecca DuFour, M.Ed., has served as a teacher, school administrator, and central office coordinator. As a former elementary principal, Becky helped her school earn state and national recognition as a model professional learning community. She is one of the featured principals in the *Video Journal of Education* program *Leadership in the Age of Standards and High Stakes* (2001). She is also the lead consultant and featured principal for the Video Journal program *Elementary Principals as Leaders of Learners* (2003). Becky is co-author of *Getting Started: Reculturing Schools to Become Professional Learning Communities* (2002) and *Whatever It Takes: How Professional Learning Communities Respond When Kids Don't Learn* (2004).

Becky has written for numerous professional journals, is a graduate of National Staff Development Council's Academy X, serves as a book reviewer for the *Journal of Staff Development,* and writes a quarterly column for the National Association of Elementary School Principals' publication *Leadership Compass.* Becky has consulted with professional organizations, school districts, universities, and state departments of education throughout North America.

Foreword

Here and Now: Improving Teaching and Learning*

Mike Schmoker

For all of the current controversy surrounding issues of student achievement and accountability, we forget that there is far less controversy about our shared desire to help more children learn, to reduce the achievement gap, and to improve the quality of the complex work of teaching in all schools, from urban to rural, from economically struggling to affluent.

So what if there was, right now, a fairly straightforward, well-established way to appreciably improve both teaching quality and levels of learning? What if evidence from numerous schools and the research community points to proven structures and practices that (1) stand to make an immediate difference in achievement and (2) require reasonable amounts of time and resources? The fact is that such structure and practice do exist and there is no reason to delay their implementation.

---

*This article is reprinted (with some changes) from *The School Administrator,* November 2004, volume 61, issue 10, pages 48–49. The author acknowledges the contributions of Richard DuFour, Carl Glickman, and Douglas Reeves in preparing this document.

A Simple Concept

There is a simple, powerful concept that we—myself and the supporters of this document, who have signed their names at the end of it—fully endorse: that of the professional learning community. It starts with a group of teachers who meet regularly as a team to identify essential and valued student learning, develop common formative assessments, analyze current levels of achievement, set achievement goals, share strategies, and then create lessons to improve upon those levels. Picture these teams of teachers implementing these new lessons, continuously assessing their results, and then adjusting their lessons in light of those results. Importantly, there must be an expectation that this collaborative effort will produce ongoing improvement and gains in achievement.

If there is anything that the research community agrees on, it is this: The right kind of continuous, structured teacher collaboration improves the quality of teaching and pays big, often immediate, dividends in student learning and professional morale in virtually any setting. Our experience with schools across the nation bears this out unequivocally.

The concurrence among researchers and practitioners in support of this conclusion is both stunning and underappreciated. Advocates for focused, structured teacher collaboration include Roland Barth, Emily Calhoun, Linda Darling-Hammond, Richard Elmore, Michael Fullan, Bruce Joyce, Judith Warren Little, Dan Lortie, Milbrey McLaughlin, Fred Newmann, Susan Rosenholtz, Rick Stiggins, James Stigler, Joan Talbert, Gary Wehlage, Grant Wiggins, Ronald Wolk, and numerous others.

Linda Darling-Hammond, a professor of teaching and teacher education at Stanford University, speaks for a legion of researchers when she writes that improvement is a function of "continual learning groups" pursuing "collective . . . explicit goals for student learning." She rightly emphasizes that success need not hinge on a school's luck in finding that rare administrator with charisma. It does, however, depend on collaborative "structures for success that maintain a press for ambitious teaching and academic achievement" (Darling-Hammond, 1997, p. 150).

Similarly, Michael Fullan, a newly appointed education adviser to the provincial government in Ontario, writes that teachers in successful schools with professional learning communities work together "on a continuing basis . . . focused on student work [through assessment]." On the basis of their assessment results, teachers then strategically "change their instructional practice accordingly to get better results" (Fullan, 2000, p. 582).

Researcher Judith Warren Little's landmark studies on this topic are definitive, but they contain an important caveat: What passes for collaboration or collegiality in schools typically lacks a focus on achievement results—on short-term formative assessment—and thus has little impact on the character and quality of teaching. Educators must not confuse mere congeniality or "collaboration lite" with the serious professional dialogue essential to school improvement.

But, like Fullan and Darling-Hammond, Little (1990) found that when teachers engage regularly in authentic "joint work" focused on explicit, common learning goals, their collaboration pays off richly in the form of higher quality solutions to instructional problems, increased teacher confidence, and, not surprisingly, remarkable gains in achievement.

Concerted Action

Mere collegiality will not cut it. Discussions about curricular issues or popular strategies can feel good but go nowhere. The right image to embrace is of a group of teachers who meet regularly to share, refine, and assess the impact of lessons and strategies continuously to help increasing numbers of students learn at higher levels.

This image—of the true professional learning community—has yet to become the norm in most schools, despite the fact that there are almost no dissenting entities on this issue, despite the contribution such joint work makes to teacher efficacy and professionalism, and despite the fact that it is neither costly nor time-consuming.

There is no good reason to delay this reform. It is time for a concerted effort to push for its inclusion in state department requirements, in every pre-service and leadership training course, and in every discussion among principals and teacher leaders that purports to improve teaching and learning.

Indeed, other factors affect achievement. But continuous, organized opportunities for collaboration and assessment that are part of an ongoing cycle of continuous improvement allow us to make the most of the best factors and strategies. These structures offer us our most practical and affordable opportunity to integrate, generate, and refine practices that influence teaching and learning.

The stakes are high, but success could redefine public education and education professions and enable us to reach unprecedented levels of quality, equity, and achievement.

Supporters (In Alphabetical Order)

Roland S. Barth is an author, educational consultant, and the Founder and Former Director of Harvard University's Principals' Center and the International Network of Principals' Centers (RSB44@aol.com).

Louis A. Castenell, Jr., is Dean and Professor, College of Education, University of Georgia, Athens (lcastene@coe.uga.edu).

Lisa D. Delpit is Eminent Scholar and Director, Center for Urban Education & Innovation, Florida International University, Miami (delpitl@fiu.edu).

Rebecca DuFour is an author and educational consultant on professional learning communities (mzprinci@charter.net).

Richard DuFour is an author and educational consultant on professional learning communities (rdufour@district125.k12.il.us).

Robert Eaker is an author and educational consultant on professional learning communities (reaker@mtsu.edu).

Barbara Eason-Watkins is an author and Chief Education Officer of the Chicago Public Schools (bewatkins@cps.k12.il.us).

Michael Fullan is an educational consultant, author, and the former Dean of the Ontario Institute for Studies in Education of the University of Toronto (mfullan@oise.utoronto.ca).

Carl D. Glickman is President, The Institute for Schools, Education, and Democracy in Athens, Georgia (isedinc@aol.com).

Asa G. Hilliard, III, is the Fuller E. Callaway Professor of Urban Education at Georgia State University, Atlanta (Ahilliard@gsu.edu).

Stephanie Hirsh is the Deputy Executive Director, National Staff Development Council (NSDCHirsh@aol.com).

Jacqueline Irvine Jordan is Candler Professor of Urban Education at Emory University in Atlanta (jirvine@learnlink.emory. edu).

Lawrence W. Lezotte is an author and the Founder of Effective Schools Products, Ltd. (www.effectiveschools.com).

Robert J. Marzano is an author and private consultant in Aurora, Colorado (robertjmarzano@aol.com).

Douglas B. Reeves is the Chairman of the Center for Performance Assessment (DBReeves@aol.com).

Jonathon Saphier is an author and the Founder and Chairman Emeritus of Teachers 21 and the Founder and President of Research for Better Teaching (RBT) (Jonathon1@aol.com).

Mike Schmoker is an educational consultant and the author of *Results: The Key to Continuous School Improvement* (schmoker@futureone.com).

Dennis Sparks is an author and the Executive Director of the National Staff Development Council (SparksNSDC@aol.com).

Rick Stiggins is an author and the Chief Executive Officer and Founder of the Assessment Training Institute (ATI) (ati@assessmentinst.com).

Tony Wagner is Co-Director of the Change Leadership Group (CLG) at the Harvard Graduate School of Education (tony_wagner@harvard.edu).

Arthur E. Wise is the President of the National Council for Accreditation of Teacher Education (art@ncate.org).

References

Darling-Hammond, L. (1997). *The right to learn.* San Francisco: Jossey-Bass.

Fullan, M. (2000). The three stories of educational reform. *Phi Delta Kappan, 81*(8), 581–584.

Little, J. W. (1990). The persistence of privacy: Autonomy and initiative in teachers' professional relations. *Teachers' College Record, 91*(4), 509–536.

On Common Ground: The Power of Professional Learning Communities

Richard DuFour, Robert Eaker, and Rebecca DuFour

Over the past several years it has been our privilege and pleasure to attend presentations and read books and articles by each of the authors whose work appears in this collection. As we listened and read, we were struck by the consistency of their message. These authors had their own particular areas of expertise, presented their ideas in their own unique ways, and had different ideas regarding the most effective strategies for bringing about significant school change. But the concepts underlying their work kept returning to the same themes. They truly seemed to stand on common ground when it came to identifying the kind of schools needed to help all students learn at high levels.

We were convinced that school practitioners who had the opportunity to explore the work of these experts would come to the same conclusion: there is a consistent message regarding the qualities of high-performing schools. We recognized, however, that most teachers and principals neither have the resources to attend professional conferences on a regular basis nor the time to devote to becoming students of the work of a variety of authors. Ultimately, we concluded that bringing the ideas of these educational leaders together into one book could be a tremendous resource for educators who are working to help their students achieve at ever-higher levels. We were thrilled when this outstanding collection of educational writers and thinkers agreed to contribute to the project.

This book is organized into five sections: "Overview of PLCs," "Critical Questions of PLCs," "Creating PLCs," "Placing PLCs in a Broader Context," and "A Call to Action." In the first section, we provide an overview by exploring the conceptual framework of professional learning communities (PLCs). The first chapter identifies the common themes that emerge throughout the book. The second chapter presents Rick's response to the question, "What is a professional learning community?" He explains that when schools function as PLCs, the educators within them embrace the premise that the fundamental purpose of the school is to see to it that all students *learn* at high levels, rather than merely be *taught* at high levels. As teachers and principals make this shift from a focus on teaching to a focus on learning, they recognize that they cannot help all students learn unless they work together collaboratively, and they constantly seek tangible evidence that students have truly acquired the intended knowledge, skills, and dispositions.

In the second section—"Critical Questions"—the authors explore the questions that drive the work of educators in learning communities. The commitment to help all students learn leads inevitably to the question, "Learn what?" In the third chapter, Douglas Reeves, the nation's most articulate proponent of clarity regarding what all students must learn, explores this question and offers advice regarding the process educators should use to clarify common standards of learning for their students. Chapter 4 delves into a second critical question: "How will we know when each student has learned?" Rick Stiggins, a leading advocate for assessments that support and encourage learning, offers powerful insights for answering that question. In chapter 5, Jonathon Saphier, one of our leading researchers on effective teaching, explores the question, "How will we respond when students don't learn?" He provides ways for individual teachers and entire schools to promote a belief in "effort-based ability" that calls for extra time and support for student learning. The section concludes with Roland Barth's cautionary tale that suggests that a school committed to student learning will produce lifelong learners rather than proficient test-takers.

Every chapter of the book offers insights into creating PLCs, but section three—"Creating PLCs"—addresses the topic very specifically. In chapter 7, Mike Schmoker, who has helped to foster a results orientation in schools as much as any writer in North America, describes what happens when teams of teachers collaboratively focus on the right issues as part of their routine work practice. Dennis Sparks, executive director of the National Staff Development Council, follows with a chapter on how leaders can shape the dialogue in their schools to foster assumptions essential to successful PLCs.

Section four—"Placing PLCs in a Broader Context"— attempts to place the PLC concept in a historical perspective and to address wide-scale implementation. In chapter 9, Larry Lezotte, a leader of Effective Schools Research, provides a historical context. He expresses satisfaction that the findings of that research have been reaffirmed throughout the years and that the PLC concept supports rather than supplants those findings. In Chapter 10, Barbara Eason-Watkins, the chief educational officer of the Chicago Public Schools, offers a frank exploration of the challenges educators face when they attempt to promote PLC concepts in schools throughout a large urban district and describes how the Chicago public school system is working to meet those challenges. In chapter 11, Michael Fullan, North America's most influential writer on the change process in schools, takes the challenge one step further by exploring a systems approach for improvement that includes schools, districts, and entire states or provinces.

The fifth section—"A Call to Action"—concludes the book with an examination of some of the reasons schools fail to implement what is clearly recognized as "best practice." More importantly, it offers suggestions for overcoming those barriers with specific, concrete actions. We hope this call to action will help schools close what has been referred to as the "knowing-doing gap."

Any listing of North America's most-respected authorities on what it takes to improve schools would include the authors you will find in this book, and it is evident that they have arrived at many of the same conclusions regarding the best strategies for raising student achievement; however, they certainly have their differences as well. For example, Mike Schmoker views small teams of teachers working collaboratively to improve the learning of their students as a powerful vehicle for school improvement. Larry Lezotte calls for a school-wide focus to the improvement initiative and prefers school-wide committees to oversee the initiative. Michael Fullan contends that the focus on individual schools will never lead to full-scale reform and insists that the effort to improve schools should be a systemic process that concentrates on districts, states, and provinces as well as on individual schools. Some of the authors cite a need for increased resources to transform schools into professional learning communities, while others suggest the transformation does not depend on resources.

Although there are some differences expressed in the chapters that follow, every author supports the premise that students would be better served if educators embraced learning rather than teaching as the mission of their school, if they worked collaboratively to help all students learn, and if they used formative assessments and a focus on results to guide their practice and foster continuous improvement. And they insist that every educator has a professional responsibility to take steps to create such schools.

It is also important to note that each of these authors has had his or her own learning enriched and extended by observing the practices of exemplary schools and the teachers and principals within them. These educators were also called upon to find common ground in the process of creating their exemplary schools. They too experienced disagreements, but ultimately they were able to focus on what united them rather than on what divided them. Like the authors of these chapters, these powerful practitioners are truly school-improvement leaders in their own right, and they represent a tremendous storehouse of collective wisdom when they are able to find common ground.

Thus, we hope that this book will accomplish several objectives. First, we hope it will be a valuable tool for educators who are doing the hard work of improving their schools. We believe this collection offers them both a coherent conceptual framework and specific, practical strategies for moving forward with their improvement efforts.

Second, we hope that it will help bridge the gap that sometimes exists between researchers and practitioners. The intended audience for these authors is not other researchers, but teachers and school administrators who are engaged in the challenges of school reform on a daily basis. Each contributor has worked closely with schools, has identified practices that have a positive impact on student learning, and now hopes to share his or her insights with educators throughout North America.

Finally, and perhaps most importantly, we hope that this book will convince faculties that they should recognize, honor, and utilize their own collective wisdom—the craft knowledge they possess that could have a tremendous impact upon student and adult learning *if* they could learn how to focus and harness that knowledge. In the final analysis, the success of each generation of students will depend not upon the knowledge of researchers and authors, but upon the collective expertise, shared commitments, and purposeful actions of the men and women who shape students' school experiences each day.

Chapter 1

Recurring Themes of Professional Learning Communities and the Assumptions They Challenge

Richard DuFour, Robert Eaker, and Rebecca DuFour

Victor Hugo once wrote, "There is one thing stronger than all the armies in the world, and that is an idea whose time has come" (Hugo, 1883–1884). Those committed to improving K–12 education should be heartened by Hugo's assertion, for there has never been greater consensus regarding the most powerful strategy for sustained, substantive school improvement. Mike Schmoker (2004) has cited "a broad, even remarkable concurrence" among educational researchers and organizational theorists who have concluded that developing the capacity of educators to function as members of professional learning communities is the "best-known means by which we might achieve truly historic, wide-scale improvements in teaching and learning" (p. 432).

Educational organizations of all varieties have also endorsed the concept of professional learning communities (PLCs). The

National Commission on Teaching and America's Future (2003), created for the expressed purpose of developing strategies for recruiting, preparing, and supporting an exemplary teaching force, concludes that "quality teaching requires strong professional learning communities" (p. 17). Five "Core Propositions" guide the National Board for Professional Teaching Standards, another organization created to advance the quality of teaching and learning. One of those propositions asserts that teachers must be members of "learning communities . . . [who] contribute to the effectiveness of their schools by working collaboratively with other professionals on instructional policy, curriculum development, and staff development" (2004). The Keys Initiative of the National Education Association (2004) was designed to help educators develop shared commitment to high academic goals, collaborative problem solving, continuous assessment for teaching and learning, and ongoing learning for professionals—critical elements of the PLC concept. The American Federation of Teachers (2004) has endorsed the premise that teachers should be engaged in a "continuous process of individual and collective examination and improvement of practice," and that staff development should be "job-embedded and site-specific"—once again, proposals consistent with the PLC concept.

The National Association of Elementary School Principals (2002) has defined the very job of elementary and middle school principals as "leading learning communities," and the National Association of Secondary School Principals (2004) has called upon its members to develop professional learning communities as one of its three key strategies to improve the learning experience of every student. The National Staff Development Council (2004) has adopted standards designed to improve the effectiveness of all schools, but the first of those standards asserts "staff development that improves learning for all students organizes adults into learning communities whose goals are aligned with the school and district."

There are many divisive issues in contemporary education. It would seem, however, that the benefits of organizing schools and districts into professional learning communities in which educators work collaboratively with and learn from one another is one idea upon which educators can find common ground. In fact, it would be difficult to identify any leading educational researcher or organization that is explicitly opposed to PLCs. Might it be said that the PLC concept is truly an idea whose time has come?

Unfortunately, an honest answer to that question is, "not so fast." Advocates of PLCs face at least three daunting challenges in their efforts to make this concept the norm in schools and districts throughout North America:

- Challenge one: Developing and applying shared knowledge

- Challenge two: Sustaining the hard work of change

- Challenge three: Transforming school culture

Challenge One: Developing and Applying Shared Knowledge

First, as Michael Fullan (2005) wisely notes, "There is a growing problem in large-scale reform; namely, the *terms* travel well, but the underlying *conceptualization and thinking* do not" (p. 10). Many schools and districts that proudly proclaim they are professional learning communities have shown little evidence of either understanding the core concepts or implementing the practices of PLCs. Educators must develop a deeper, shared knowledge of learning community concepts and practices, and then must demonstrate the discipline to apply those concepts and practices in their own settings if their schools are to be transformed.

Challenge Two: Sustaining the Hard Work of Change

The second challenge flows from the first. It has been said that even the grandest design eventually degenerates into hard work. The PLC concept may be the most powerful design to improve schools, but it will require more than adopting new mission statements, launching strategic plans, or flying a banner proclaiming "we are a learning community" to develop the capacity of educators to create PLCs. Administrators and teachers, whose plates are already full, will be called upon to do the hard work associated with significant school reform. And it does take hard work. Although educators in schools that are functioning as PLCs typically report that their load has been lightened by the clarity, collaborative culture, and collective responsibility in their schools, they also acknowledge that it did require considerable effort and energy to break from old habits and to begin to act in new ways.

In his landmark study, Jim Collins (2001) found that the success of organizations that were able to make the leap from "good to great" was never the result of a single defining action, groundbreaking program, or miracle moment. As Collins wrote:

> Good to great comes by a cumulative process—
> step by step, action by action, decision by decision, turn upon turn of the flywheel—that adds up to sustained and spectacular results. . . . It was a quiet, deliberate process of figuring out what needed to be done to create the best future

results and then taking those steps one way or the other. By pushing in a constant direction over an extended period of time, they inevitably hit a point of breakthrough. (p. 169)

Educators can create professional learning communities, but there are no easy shortcuts for doing so. It will require a staff to find common ground and to exert a focused, coherent, consistent effort over time.

Challenge Three: Transforming School Culture

The third challenge is even more problematic. With no disrespect to Monsieur Hugo, even an idea whose time seems to have come can lose momentum when colliding with the traditional beliefs it challenges, particularly if those beliefs continue to go largely unexamined.

The PLC concept represents more than just a series of practices—it rests upon a set of beliefs, assumptions, and expectations regarding school.

Therefore, significant school transformation will require more than changes in structure—the policies, programs, and procedures of a school. Substantive and lasting change will ultimately require a transformation of culture—the beliefs, assumptions, expectations, and habits that constitute the norm for the people throughout the organization. Principals and teachers can be placed in new structures and go through the motions of new practices, but unless they eventually develop new competencies and new commitments that lead to true school reculturing, they will continue to be under the inexorable pull of their traditional practices and the assumptions that drive them. If schools are to be successful in developing their capacity as PLCs, new assumptions must ultimately prevail over long-standing traditional beliefs.

Let's examine the recurring themes that will emerge from the various authors who have contributed to this book as well as the traditional assumptions with which those themes are likely to collide.

Clashing Purposes: Learning for All Versus Teaching for All

The authors of the chapters in this collection repeatedly ground their proposals for substantive school reform on the premise that the very purpose of schooling is to ensure that all students acquire the knowledge, skills, and dispositions essential to their future success. Their emphasis is not on raising test scores, but on schools making a positive difference in the lives of students and thereby fulfilling a fundamentally moral purpose.

Their premise—that schools exist to ensure that all students *learn* at high levels—collides with the traditional assumption that the purpose of school is to ensure that students are *taught*. When the latter assumption prevails, educators believe they have a responsibility to give all students the opportunity to learn, but the extent of the learning will depend on factors outside the school's sphere of influence, such as innate ability, students' socioeconomic levels, their degree of motivation, and so on.

The institutions in which contemporary educators work were built upon the premise that the ability to achieve high levels of learning was reserved for the elite, and that schools served students and society best by sorting and selecting students based upon their ability to learn and their likely occupations. Even the most enlightened thinkers who led the initiative to create public schooling accepted this premise. For example, Thomas Jefferson called for Virginia schools to educate all children for 3 years, and then begin a carefully designed process of elimination that would limit the number of students eligible to attend college to no more than 10 males each year (Jefferson, 1782). The early advocates of public high school designed the institution to sort and select students, arguing that all students "cannot do and do not need the same education" (Leavitt, 1912, p. 2). The National Education Association officially endorsed this premise, criticizing the "excessively democratic ideal that all are equal and our society is devoid of classes" (Cubberly, 1909, p. 57) and applauding the recognition of "differences among children as to aptitude, interests, economic resources, and prospective careers" (National Education Association, 1910, p. 96).

The working class did not rally around the high school as an institution designed to promote educational opportunity for their children. In fact, the most powerful labor union of the late 19th Century opposed public high schools as "class education" for which only the beneficiaries should pay (Welter, 1963). In the early 20th Century, university presidents throughout the United States complained that too many students were being admitted to college at a time when only 3.3% of the nation had earned a college degree (Cremin, 1964). Dropping out of high school prior to graduation was the norm in the United States until the 1950s. Clearly, the idea that all students could or should learn at high levels was inconceivable to earlier generations, and they designed their institutions to reflect their basic assumption that intelligence was something you were born with, not something you acquired.

The legacy of this assumption continues to have significant influence upon the policies and practices of contemporary schools, and, more importantly, the lives of the students who attend them. But sorting and selecting students has never come at a higher cost. A recent analysis (Mortenson, 2004) of the impact of higher education upon earning power concluded:

> Since about 1973 a college education has become the most direct path to well paid employment and financial security in the United States. Until the early 1970s one could achieve a middle-class lifestyle by being honest and working hard. But over the last 30 years a college education has become a requisite addition. . . . A high school education or less is no longer sufficient and has not been so for three decades.

This finding is particularly sobering in light of the fact that educational attainment continues to be heavily influenced by family income, with those in the top income quartile ten times more likely to earn a college degree than those in the bottom quartile (American Youth Policy Forum, 2001).

Peter Drucker (1992) contends that the first and most significant question the members of any organization must answer if they hope to improve its effectiveness is the question of purpose. What is the task we have been organized to accomplish? If the purpose of schooling is to ensure that all students are taught, and then to assist in the sorting and selecting process based on the initial academic success or the perceived aptitude of students, there is no compelling reason to improve schools. In fact, it could be argued that schools have been tremendously effective in fulfilling their purpose of sorting and selecting students.

If, however, as Doug Reeves writes so persuasively in chapter 3, the fundamental purpose of schooling is to ensure that all students acquire the knowledge, skills, and dispositions essential to their success as ongoing learners, the need for improvement is immediate and imperative. The PLC concept is grounded in this making-a-difference sense of moral purpose, but if the PLC model is to take root in school, it must supplant the deeply entrenched traditional assumptions that have guided schools for over a century.

In his study of high-performing organizations, Jim Collins (2001) found that those organizations simplified a complex world into a single organizing idea, a basic principle, or a concept that unified and guided the work of everyone within the organization. In a PLC, that unifying principle asserts that we have not fulfilled our fundamental purpose until *all* students have learned at high levels. Once that principle is truly embraced, the need for significant change becomes evident. Educators begin to work together to clarify such questions as:

- What is it we want all students to learn?

- How will we know when each student has mastered the essential learning?

- How will we respond when a student experiences initial difficulty in learning?

- How will we deepen the learning for students who have already mastered essential knowledge and skills?

When educators embrace learning for all as the fundamental purpose of their school, they begin to recognize that some students will require additional time and support in order to be successful, and they develop processes for providing that time and support during the school day on a timely, directive, and systematic basis. They shift their focus from summative assessments to formative assessments. They compare each student's performance to an agreed-upon standard rather than comparing students to each other. They concentrate on each student's mastery of each essential knowledge and skill rather than relying on averages. They recognize the need to work together collaboratively rather than in isolation. In short, as Andy Hargreaves (2004) observes, "A professional learning community is an ethos that infuses every single aspect of a school's operation. When a school becomes a professional learning community, everything in the school looks different than it did before" (p. 5).

But in order for this transformation to occur, the idea that schools were created to ensure all students must learn at high levels must ultimately prevail. As Edward Fiske (1992), the long-time educational correspondent of the *New York Times*, wrote, "to truly reform American Education we must abandon the long-standing assumption that the central activity is teaching and reorient all policy making and activities around a new benchmark: student learning" (p. 253).

Collaborative Cultures Versus Teacher Isolation

A second major idea embedded in the PLC concept and a theme that emerges repeatedly throughout this book is that educators cannot help all students learn at high levels unless they work together collaboratively. The research in support of the benefits of collaboration is exhaustive, as is the research that links collaborative cultures to improving schools. Yet, despite the abundance of evidence regarding the benefits of collaborative cultures and the virtual absence of evidence to the contrary, it is the norm for public school teachers in North America to work in isolation with individual teachers, like independent subcontractors, teaching discrete groups of students. An honest assessment of the brutal facts in most schools would support Tracy Kidder's (1989) observation: "Decades of research and reform have not altered the fundamental facts of teaching. The task of universal, public education is still being conducted by a woman alone in a little room, presiding over a youthful distillate of a town or city" (p. 53).

Seymour Sarason (1996) laments that almost 40 years ago he described teaching as "a lonely profession," and little has changed. A landmark sociological study of teaching conducted over a quarter of a century ago described its "cellular structure" in which each teacher assumes responsibility for his or her own room and own students (Lortie, 1975), a description that still rings true today.

Why has the isolation prevailed despite the evidence that it serves the interests of neither students nor teachers? Is it, as Bruce Joyce (2004) suggests, because the profession attracts people who are specifically seeking workplaces of high isolation? Or is it, as Sarason contends, that the structure and culture of schools create such physical and psychological isolation of teachers that it is almost impossible for them to engage in productive learning with their colleagues? Is it the influence of higher education where academic freedom has been revered and individual autonomy has been regarded as a professional perquisite? Is it the influence of the media whose sympathetic portrayal of a teacher inevitably depicts the courageous individual working alone against the system and the bureaucratic administrators who perpetuate it (think *Goodbye Mr. Chips, To*

Sir With Love, Dangerous Minds, Stand and Deliver)? Or is it simply because it is far easier to work alone than to learn together? Regardless of the reason for the undeniable endurance of teacher isolation, the PLC concept will never become the norm in schools unless educators take steps to (1) systematically embed collaboration in the routine practices of the school and, just as importantly, (2) provide the structure and parameters to ensure that the collaboration focuses on improving the learning of both students and adults. Despite the overwhelming evidence of the benefits of a collaborative culture, the tradition of teacher isolation continues to pose a formidable barrier to those hoping to implement PLC concepts in their schools.

Collective Capacity Versus Individual Development

The PLC concept is specifically designed to develop the collective capacity of a staff to work together to achieve the fundamental purpose of the school: high levels of learning for all students. Leaders of the process purposefully set out to create the conditions that enable teachers to learn from one another as part of their routine work practices. Continuous learning becomes school based and job embedded. In chapter 10, Barbara Eason-Watkins describes this focus on building the collective capacity of a staff as the linchpin strategy for promoting PLCs throughout the entire Chicago public school system.

This new vision of professional development—building the collective capacity of a staff to achieve its goals through job-embedded learning—flies in the face of traditional staff development. Two of the byproducts of the isolation of teachers have been that the individual classroom teacher has typically been the focus of school improvement efforts and that the source of professional development has been seen as external—something that occurs away from the school or when someone from outside the school drops in to share some wisdom. Individual teachers traditionally have been provided with incentives to pursue their personal professional development away from the school—tuition support for graduate courses, movement on the salary schedule for advanced degrees, funding for workshops and conferences, and so on. The underlying assumption behind this approach is that if the third grade teacher becomes a better teacher in his or her "cellular structure" (that is, private kingdom), the school will become more effective in achieving its goals.

This premise—the development of individuals ensures enhanced organizational performance—is patently wrong. In their landmark study of successful schools, Newmann and his associates (1996) found that leaders of those schools realized that increasing the knowledge and skills of individual teachers was not sufficient to foster sustained school improvement. They focused instead on "increasing the capacity of the organization by placing issues of teaching and learning at the center of the dialogue among the entire school community" (p. 291). And building collective capacity requires more than sending teachers off to pursue different courses or providing them with workshops. As Michael Fullan (2005) wrote, "capacity building . . . is the daily habit of *working together,* and you can't learn this from a workshop or course. You need to learn it by doing it and getting better at it on purpose" (p. 69).

The best professional development occurs in the context of the workplace rather than the workshop as teachers work together to address the issues and challenges that are relevant to them. It is pursued in a social setting with opportunities for interaction rather than in isolation. It is directly and purposefully designed to help educators accomplish the collective goals of their team and school rather than having individuals pursue their personal interests and agendas. Until the conceptual model that guides the professional development of a staff becomes teams of teachers working together in the context of their school to develop the knowledge and skills necessary to achieve their team and school goals, that school will have difficulty becoming a PLC.

A Focus on Results Versus a Focus on Activities

Of course, once the focus of professional development shifts from the individual staff member to improving the school's collective capacity to fulfill its purpose and achieve its goals, the school begins to develop a results orientation. Educators begin to ask, "What evidence do we have that this initiative or this practice is helping us to become more effective in assisting all students to achieve at high levels?" As Peter Senge and his associates (1994) observe, "ultimately, a learning organization is judged by results" (p. 44).

Traditionally, however, schools have demonstrated "almost a cultural and ingrained aversion to reckoning with much less living with results" (Schmoker, 1996, p. 3). Several factors have contributed to this aversion. First, schools continue to operate under the old factory model that assumes if the inputs are correct—if teachers are provided with the right curriculum, the right textbook, the right schedule, and so on—the results will take care of themselves.

Second, many educators have confused activity or "busyness" with results. This tendency is particularly evident in

"Christmas tree schools"—schools that pursue every new fad so that it can be added, like an ornament, to the structure of the school. Unfortunately, ornaments are fragile, likely to be dislodged by the first ill wind, and never become organic. They may be *on* the tree, but they are not *of* the tree.

Finally, some educators are content with the nobility of their cause and are prone to substitute good intentions for results. Intentions are fine, but they will not impact results unless and until they are translated into specific concrete actions and collective commitments. Can educators overcome their traditional tendencies to focus on activity and inputs and, as Jim Collins urges all those who hope to build great institutions, become "fanatically driven, infected with an incurable need to produce *results*" (2001)?

Assessment for Learning Versus Assessment of Learning

One of the most consistent (and profound) messages presented in this collection of leading educational authors is that assessment, when done well, can be a powerful catalyst for improved learning on the part of both the students and the adults within a school. They endorse Rick Stiggin's idea of "assessment *for* learning"—assessments that are used both to identify students who need additional support and to inform teacher practice. The authors describe teachers within a grade-level or course working together to build common assessments of essential learning. These assessments are timely; they give teachers and students frequent, ongoing feedback on the extent of each student's learning. They are standards based; they help teachers answer the question, "How do we know if each of our students is acquiring the knowledge and skills we intended?" The assessments are formative; they are used as tools to identify where a student might be experiencing difficulty so that the student can receive additional time and support until he or she has mastered the skill. The data from these common formative assessments are easily accessible and openly shared between teachers who then assist each other in addressing areas of concern. One of the most significant tools available to a school that is attempting to build a PLC is this process of clarifying essential outcomes, building common assessments, reaching consensus on the criteria by which teachers will judge the quality of student work, and working together to analyze data and improve results.

Unfortunately, this process faces formidable barriers in traditional schools. School-based assessments have been left to the discretion of individual teachers rather than developed by a collaborative team of colleagues. The idea of sharing their students' results with their peers (and perhaps exposing a weakness in their teaching) is not readily embraced by teachers who have spent their lives working in isolation. Teachers have tended to attribute variations in student achievement to differences in student ability rather than the effectiveness of their instruction, and thus have not viewed assessments as a way to inform their professional practice. Furthermore, as Rick Stiggins notes, the history of testing in the United States has reflected the original purpose of sorting and selecting students. Tests were not designed to help students learn; they were designed to differentiate between students (such as nationally normed tests) or to reward and punish students (summative tests). Assumptions about testing are well entrenched in many public schools, and advocates of PLCs will need to confront those assumptions if the PLC concept is to prevail.

Widespread Leadership Versus the Charismatic Leader

The PLC concept operates from the premise that leadership should be widely dispersed throughout a school, and thus developing the leadership potential of all staff members is imperative. Principals in PLCs are called upon to regard themselves as leaders of leaders rather than leaders of followers, and broadening teacher leadership becomes one of their priorities. In fact, The National Commission on Teaching and America's Future (2003, p. 17) concluded that "shared or distributive leadership" was essential to building learning communities.

The importance of widely dispersed leadership is echoed in the research outside of education as well. As one extensive study of leadership concluded, "Leadership is not a solo act. In the thousands of personal-best leadership cases we studied, we have yet to encounter a single example of extraordinary achievement that occurred without the active involvement and support of many people. Fostering collaboration is the route to high performance" (Kouzes & Posner, 1996, p. 106).

Yet schools continue to search for the charismatic, heroic leader who will single-handedly ride in to rescue a demoralized or inept staff—and they make frequent changes in leadership when the individual fails to demonstrate that he or she is the all-knowing visionary who can point the way to those who are less capable. Peter Senge and associates (1994) contend this traditional view of leaders as heroes—as people who set the direction, make the decisions, and energize the troops—is deeply rooted in the individualistic worldview of the West. As he writes, "At its heart, this traditional view of leadership is based on assumptions of people's powerlessness, their lack of personal vision and inability to master the forces of change, deficits which can be remedied only by a few great leaders" (p. 340).

The myth persists despite evidence to the contrary. In their research on professional learning communities, McLaughlin and Talbert (2001) reported, "We encountered no instances to support the 'great leader theory,' charismatic people who create extraordinary contexts for teaching by virtue of their unique vision. . . . [Effective] principals empower and support teacher leadership to improve teaching practice" (p. 118).

In the private sector there is considerable evidence that there is a *negative* correlation between charismatic leadership and sustained organizational excellence (Collins & Porras, 1997). As long as schools cling to the idea of the leader as the source of inspiration and energy, their efforts to improve will continue to be characterized by stops and starts as leaders come and go. To become a PLC, a school must transcend its dependence on a single leader and develop a culture that sustains improvement despite the departure of key individuals.

Self-Efficacy Versus Dependency

If there is a single theme that unites the chapters of this book and the authors who wrote them, it is that educators are capable of helping more students achieve at higher levels than ever before. In chapter 11, Michael Fullan contends that highly effective schools will remain serendipitous anomalies rather than the norm unless districts, states, and provinces engage in systemic reform to support professional learning communities. It is important to note, however, that he also emphasizes the need for individual educators to contribute to that systemic change by taking immediate steps to improve their schools. As he writes, "Each of us *is* the system."

There are hundreds, if not thousands, of schools that have used the themes we outline in this chapter to help their students achieve at higher levels. We can point to schools at all levels—elementary, middle, and high schools; large and small schools; suburban, rural, and urban schools; schools of affluence and schools of poverty—that have successfully implemented PLC concepts and experienced gains in student achievement. Ron Edmonds (1979) once asked a chilling question: "How many effective schools would you have to see to be persuaded of the educability of all children?" (p. 24). The evidence of such schools is now so pervasive that no fair-minded person could refute what Edmonds and Larry Lezotte asserted almost 40 years ago: the practices of educators—what we do in our schools—can have a positive impact on student learning. Educators within a PLC are willing to acknowledge that many of the factors that result in improved student learning do lie within their sphere of influence.

In chapter 5, Jonathon Saphier makes a compelling case for the importance of teaching students to believe in "effort-based ability"—the sense of self-efficacy that convinces students that their success is dependent upon their effort, commitment, and tenacity rather than factors outside of their control. But of course the best way to instill that belief in students is to model it as adults. Will educators be able to move from an "if only" culture (if only we had more resources, if only the kids were motivated) to a "can do" culture? Will they be able to acknowledge that they have helped to create many of the barriers to high levels of learning for all? Roland Barth (1991) did a wonderful job of presenting that question almost 15 years ago when he asked principals and teachers if they were willing to:

> . . . accept the fact that they are part of the prob-
> lem rather than the helpless victims of cultural

circumstances. God didn't create self-contained classrooms, fifty-minute periods, subjects taught in isolation. *We* did—because we find working alone safer than and preferable to working together. . . . We *can* work to change the embedded structures so that our schools become more hospitable places for student and adult learning. But little will really change unless we change *ourselves.* (p. 128)

If schools are to be transformed into professional learning communities, the educators within them will be required to change many things—including themselves. The authors of these chapters will provide readers with a powerful conceptual framework and specific proven strategies for building PLCs, but in the final analysis, those concepts and strategies will be brought to life only if educators begin to do differently—to take actions consistent with the belief that it is their job to help all students learn at high levels, to discontinue practices and procedures that are not aligned with that purpose, and to demonstrate an unwavering faith that regardless of the difficulties, they will prevail in the end.

References

American Federation of Teachers. (2004). Professional development for teachers. Retrieved November 15, 2004, from http://www.aft.org/topics/teacher-quality/prodev.htm.

American Youth Policy Forum. (2001). The forgotten half revisited: American youth and young families, 1988–2008. Retrieved November 15, 2004, from www.ecs.org/clearinghouse/26/81/2681.htm.

Barth, R. (1991). Restructuring schools: Some questions for teachers and principals. *Phi Delta Kappan, 73*(2), 123–128.

Collins, J. (2001). *Good to great: Why some companies make the leap . . . and others don't.* New York: Harper Business.

Collins, J., & Porras, J. (1997). *Built to last: Successful habits of visionary companies.* New York: Harper Business.

Cremin, L. (1964). *The transformation of the school: Progressivism in American education.* New York: Alfred Knopf.

Cubberly, E. (1909). *Changing conceptions of education.* Boston: Houghton-Mifflin.

Drucker, P. (1992). *Managing for the future: The 1990s and beyond.* New York: Talley Books.

DuFour, R. (2002). The learning-centered principal. *Educational Leadership, 59*(8), 12–15.

DuFour, R., DuFour, R., Eaker, R., & Karhanek, G. (2004). *Whatever it takes: How professional learning communities respond when kids don't learn.* Bloomington, IN: Solution Tree (formerly National Educational Service).

DuFour, R., & Eaker, R. (1998). *Professional learning communities at work: Best practices to enhance student achievement.* Bloomington, IN: Solution Tree (formerly National Educational Service).

Edmonds, R. (1979). Effective schools for the urban poor. *Educational Leadership, 37*(18), 20–24.

Fiske, E. (1992). *Smart schools: Smart kids. Why do some schools work?* New York: Simon and Schuster.

Fullan, M. (2005). *Leadership and sustainability: Systems thinkers in action.* Thousand Oaks, CA: Corwin Press.

Hargreaves, A. (2004). Broader purpose calls for higher understanding: An interview with Andy Hargreaves. *Journal of Staff Development, 5*(2), 46–50.

Hugo, V. (1883–1884). *Histoire d'un crime.* Paris: J. Hetzel & cie. Quote retrieved January 11, 2005, from http://quotations.about.com/cs/inspirationquotes/a/Business6.htm

Jefferson, T. (1782). Bill on Education. Thomas Jefferson Digital Archive Number 2398. Charlottesville, VA: University of Virginia Library. Retrieved March 19, 2004, from http://etext.lib.virginia.edu/etcbin/foleydate-browse?id=1782.

Joyce, B. (2004). How are professional learning communities created? History has a few messages. *Phi Delta Kappan, 86*(1), 76–83.

Kidder, T. (1989). *Among school children.* Boston: Houghton Mifflin.

Kouzes, J., & Posner, B. (1996). Seven lessons for leading the voyage to the future. In F. Hesselbein, M. Goldsmith, & R. Beckhard (Eds.), *The leader of the future.* San Francisco: Jossey-Bass.

Leavitt, F. (1912). *Examples of an industrial education.* Boston: Ginn and Company.

Lortie, D. (1975). *Schoolteacher.* Chicago: University of Chicago.

McLaughlin, M., & Talbert, J. (2001). *Professional learning communities and the work of high school teaching.* Chicago: University of Chicago Press.

The Mortenson Research Seminar on Public Policy. (2004). Postsecondary education opportunity. Retrieved November 15, 2004, from www.ecs.org/clearinghouse/26/81/2681.htm.

National Association of Elementary School Principals. (2002). *Leading learning communities: Standards for what principals should know and be able to do.* Alexandria, VA: Author.

National Association of Secondary School Principals. (2004). Breaking ranks II: Strategies for leading high school reform. Reston, VA: Author.

National Board of Professional Teaching Standards. (2004). What teachers should know and be able to do: The five core propositions. Retrieved November 15, 2004, from http://www.nbpts.org/about/coreprops.cfm#prop5.

National Commission on Teaching and America's Future. (2003). *No dream denied: A pledge to America's children. Summary report.* Washington, DC: Author.

National Education Association. (1910). Report of the Commission on the Place of Industries in Public Education. (1974). In M. Lazerson & W. N. Grubbs (Eds.), *American education and vocationalism: A documentary history.* New York: Teachers College Press.

National Education Association. (2004). School quality. Retrieved November 15, 2004, from http://www.nea.org/schoolquality.

National Staff Development Council. (2004). *Tools for growing the NSDC Standards.* Oxford, OH: Author.

Newmann, F., and Associates. (1996). *Authentic achievement: Restructuring schools for intellectual quality.* San Francisco: Jossey-Bass.

Sarason, S. (1996). *Revisiting the culture of the school and the problem of change.* New York: Teachers College.

Schmoker, M. (1996). *Results: The key to continuous school improvement.* Alexandria, VA: Association of Supervision and Curriculum Development.

Schmoker, M. (2004). Tipping point: From feckless reform to substantive instructional improvement. *Phi Delta Kappan. 85*(6), 424–432.

Senge, P., Ross, R., Smith, B., Roberts, C., & Kleiner, A. (1994). *The fifth discipline fieldbook: Strategies and tools for building a learning organization.* New York: Doubleday.

Welter, R. (1963). *Popular education and democratic thought.* New York: Columbia University Press.

Chapter 2

What Is a Professional Learning Community?*

Richard DuFour

The idea of improving schools by developing professional learning communities is becoming more and more popular. But people use this term to describe every imaginable combination of individuals with an interest in education—a grade-level teaching team, a school committee, a high school department, an entire school district, a state department of education, a national professional organization, and so on. In fact, the term has been used so ubiquitously that it is in danger of losing all meaning.

The professional learning community model has now reached a critical juncture, one well known to those who have witnessed the fate of other well-intentioned school reform efforts. In this all-too-familiar cycle, initial enthusiasm gives way to confusion about the fundamental concepts driving the

*This article is reprinted (with some changes) from *Educational Leadership,* May 2004, volume 61, issue 8, pages 6–11. *Educational Leadership* is published by the Association for Supervision and Curriculum Development (ASCD).

initiative, followed by inevitable implementation problems, the conclusion that the reform has failed to bring about the desired results, abandonment of the reform, and the launch of a new search for the next promising initiative. Another reform movement has come and gone, reinforcing the conventional education wisdom that promises, "This too shall pass."

The movement to develop professional learning communities can avoid this cycle, but only if educators reflect critically on the concept's merits. What are the big ideas that represent the core principles of professional learning communities? How do these principles guide schools' efforts to sustain the professional learning community model until it becomes deeply embedded in the culture of the school?

Big Idea #1: Ensuring That Students Learn

The professional learning community model flows from the assumption that the core mission of formal education is not simply to ensure that students are taught but to ensure that they learn. This simple shift—from a focus on teaching to a focus on learning—has profound implications for schools.

School mission statements that promise "learning for all" have become a cliché. But when a school staff takes that statement literally—when teachers view it as a pledge to ensure the success of each student rather than as politically correct hyperbole—profound changes begin to take place. The school staff finds itself asking, "What school characteristics and practices have been most successful in helping all students achieve at high levels? How could we adopt those characteristics and practices in our own school? What commitments would we have to make to one another to create such a school? What indicators could we monitor to assess our progress?" When the staff has built shared knowledge and found common ground on these questions, the school has a solid foundation for moving forward with its improvement initiative.

As the school moves forward, every professional in the building must engage with colleagues in the ongoing exploration of three crucial questions that drive the work of those within a professional learning community:

- What do we want each student to learn?

- How will we know when each student has learned it?

- How will we respond when a student experiences difficulty in learning?

The answer to the third question separates learning communities from traditional schools.

Here is a scenario that plays out daily in traditional schools. A teacher teaches a unit to the best of his or her ability, but at the conclusion of the unit some students have not mastered the essential outcomes. On the one hand, the teacher would like to take the time to help those students. On the other hand, the teacher feels compelled to move forward to cover the course content. If the teacher uses instructional time to assist students who have not learned, the progress of students who have mastered the content will suffer; if the teacher pushes on with new concepts, the struggling students will fall farther behind.

What typically happens in this situation? Almost invariably, the school leaves the solution to the discretion of individual teachers, who vary widely in the ways they respond. Some teachers conclude that the struggling students should transfer to a less rigorous course or should be considered for special education. Some lower their expectations by adopting less challenging standards for subgroups of students within their classrooms. Some look for ways to assist the students before and after school. Some allow struggling students to fail.

When a school begins to function as a professional learning community, however, teachers become aware of the incongruity between their commitment to ensure learning for all students and their lack of a coordinated strategy to respond when some students do not learn. The staff addresses this discrepancy by designing strategies to ensure that struggling students receive additional time and support, no matter who their teacher is. In addition to being systematic and schoolwide, the professional learning community's response to students who experience difficulty is

- *Timely*. The school quickly identifies students who need additional time and support.

- *Based on intervention rather than remediation*. The plan provides students with help as soon as they experience difficulty rather than relying on summer school, retention, and remedial courses.

- *Directive*. Instead of *inviting* students to seek additional help, the systematic plan *requires* students to devote extra time and receive additional assistance until they have mastered the necessary concepts.

The systematic, timely, and directive intervention program operating at Adlai Stevenson High School in Lincolnshire, Illinois, provides an excellent example. Every 3 weeks, every student receives a progress report. Within the first month of school, new students discover that if they are not doing well in a class, they will receive a wide array of immediate interventions. First, the teacher, counselor, and faculty advisor each talk with the student individually to help resolve the problem. The school also notifies the student's parents about the concern. In addition, the school offers the struggling student a pass from study hall to a school tutoring center to get additional help in the course. An older student mentor, in conjunction with the struggling student's advisor, helps the student with homework during the student's daily advisory period.

Any student who continues to fall short of expectations at the end of 6 weeks despite these interventions is required, rather than invited, to attend tutoring sessions during the study hall period. Counselors begin to make weekly checks on the struggling student's progress. If tutoring fails to bring about improvement within the next 6 weeks, the student is assigned to a daily guided study hall with 10 or fewer students. The guided study hall supervisor communicates with classroom teachers to learn exactly what homework each student needs to complete and monitors the completion of that homework. Parents attend a meeting at the school at which the student, parents, counselor, and classroom teacher must sign a contract clarifying what each party will do to help the student meet the standards for the course.

Stevenson High School serves more than 4,000 students. Yet this school has found a way to monitor each student's learning on a timely basis and to ensure that every student who experiences academic difficulty will receive extra time and support for learning.

Like Stevenson, schools that are truly committed to the concept of learning for each student will stop subjecting struggling students to a haphazard education lottery. These schools will guarantee that each student receives whatever additional support he or she needs.

Big Idea #2: A Culture of Collaboration

Educators who are building a professional learning community recognize that they must work together to achieve their collective purpose of learning for all. Therefore, they create structures to promote a collaborative culture.

Despite compelling evidence indicating that working collaboratively represents best practice, teachers in many schools continue to work in isolation. Even in schools that endorse the idea of collaboration, the staff's willingness to collaborate often stops at the classroom door. Some school staffs equate the term "collaboration" with congeniality and focus on building group camaraderie. Other staffs join forces to develop consensus on operational procedures, such as how they will respond to tardiness or supervise recess. Still others organize themselves into committees to oversee different facets of the school's operation, such as discipline, technology, and social climate. Although each of these activities can serve a useful purpose, none represents the kind of professional dialogue that can transform a school into a professional learning community.

The powerful collaboration that characterizes professional learning communities is a systematic process in which teachers work together to analyze and improve their classroom practice. Teachers work in teams, engaging in an ongoing cycle of questions that promote deep team learning. This process, in turn, leads to higher levels of student achievement.

Collaborating for school improvement. At Boones Mill Elementary School, a K–5 school serving 400 students in rural Franklin County, Virginia, the powerful collaboration of grade-level teams drives the school improvement process. The following scenario describes what Boones Mill staff members refer to as their *team learning process*.

The school's five third grade teachers study state and national standards, the district curriculum guide, and student achievement data to identify the essential knowledge and skills that all students should learn in an upcoming language arts unit. They also ask the fourth grade teachers what they hope students will have mastered by the time they leave third grade. On the basis of the shared knowledge generated by this joint study, the third grade team agrees on the critical outcomes that they will make sure each student achieves during the unit.

Next, the team turns its attention to developing common formative assessments to monitor each student's mastery of the essential outcomes. Team members discuss the most authentic and valid ways to assess student mastery. They set the standard for each skill or concept that each student must achieve to be deemed proficient. They agree on the criteria by which they will judge the quality of student work, and they practice applying those criteria until they can do so consistently. Finally, they decide when they will administer the assessments.

After each teacher has examined the results of the common formative assessment for his or her students, the team analyzes how all third graders performed. Team members identify strengths and weaknesses in student learning and begin to discuss how they can build on the strengths and address the weaknesses. The entire team gains new insights into what is working and what is not, and members discuss new strategies that they can implement in their classrooms to raise student achievement.

At Boones Mill, collaborative conversations happen routinely throughout the year. Teachers use frequent formative assessments to investigate the questions "Are students learning what they need to learn?" and "Who needs additional time and support to learn?" rather than relying solely on summative assessments that ask "Which students learned what was intended and which students did not?"

Collaborative conversations call on team members to make public what has traditionally been private—goals, strategies, materials, pacing, questions, concerns, and results. These discussions give every teacher someone to turn to and talk to, and they are explicitly structured to improve the classroom practice of teachers—individually and collectively.

For teachers to participate in such a powerful process, the school must ensure that everyone belongs to a team that focuses on student learning. Each team must have time to meet during the workday and throughout the school year. Teams must focus their efforts on crucial questions related to learning and generate products that reflect that focus, such as lists of essential outcomes, different kinds of assessment, analyses of student achievement, and strategies for improving results. Teams must develop norms or protocols to clarify expectations regarding roles, responsibilities, and relationships among team members. Teams must adopt student achievement goals linked with school and district goals.

Removing barriers to success. For meaningful collaboration to occur, a number of things must also *stop* happening. Schools must stop pretending that merely presenting teachers with state standards or district curriculum guides will guarantee that all students have access to a common curriculum. Even school districts that devote tremendous time and energy to designing the *intended* curriculum often pay little attention to the *implemented* curriculum (what teachers actually teach) and even less to the *attained* curriculum (what students learn) (Marzano, 2003). Schools must also give teachers time to analyze and discuss state and district curriculum documents. More important, teacher conversations must quickly move beyond "What are we expected to teach?" to "How will we know when each student has learned?"

In addition, faculties must stop making excuses for failing to collaborate. Few educators publicly assert that working in isolation is the best strategy for improving schools. Instead, they give reasons why it is impossible for them to work together: "We just can't find the time." "Not everyone on the staff has endorsed the idea." "We need more training in collaboration." But the number of schools that have created truly collaborative cultures proves that such barriers are not insurmountable.

In the final analysis, building the collaborative culture of a professional learning community is a question of will. A group of staff members who are determined to work together will find a way.

Big Idea #3: A Focus on Results

Professional learning communities judge their effectiveness on the basis of results. Working together to improve student achievement becomes the routine work of everyone in the school. Every teacher team participates in an ongoing process of identifying the current level of student achievement, establishing a goal to improve the current level, working together to achieve that goal, and providing periodic evidence of progress. The focus of team goals shifts. Such goals as "We will adopt the Junior Great Books program" or "We will create three new labs for our science course" give way to "We will increase the percentage of students who meet the state standard in language arts from 83% to 90%" or "We will reduce the failure rate in our course by 50%."

Schools and teachers typically suffer from the DRIP syndrome—Data Rich/Information Poor. The results-oriented professional learning community not only welcomes data but also turns data into useful and relevant information for staff. Teachers have never suffered from a lack of data. Even a teacher who works in isolation can easily establish the mean, mode, median, standard deviation, and percentage of students who demonstrate proficiency every time he or she administers a test. However, data will become a catalyst for improved teacher practice only if the teacher has a basis of comparison.

When teacher teams develop common formative assessments throughout the school year, each teacher can identify how his or her students performed on each skill compared with other students. Individual teachers can call on their team colleagues to help them reflect on areas of concern. Each teacher has access to the ideas, materials, strategies, and talents of the entire team.

Freeport Intermediate School, located 50 miles south of Houston, Texas, attributes its success to an unrelenting focus on results. Teachers work in collaborative teams for 90 minutes daily to clarify the essential outcomes of their grade levels and courses and to align those outcomes with state standards.

They develop consistent instructional calendars and administer the same brief assessment to all students in the same grade level at the conclusion of each instructional unit, roughly once a week.

Each quarter, the teams administer a common cumulative exam. Each spring, the teams develop and administer practice tests for the state exam. Each year, the teams pore over the results of the state test, which are broken down to show every teacher how his or her students performed on every skill and on every test item. The teachers share their results from all of these assessments with their colleagues, and they quickly learn when a teammate has been particularly effective in teaching a certain skill. Team members consciously look for successful practice and attempt to replicate it in their own practice; they also identify areas of the curriculum that need more attention.

Freeport Intermediate has been transformed from one of the lowest-performing schools in the state to a national model for academic achievement. Principal Clara Sale-Davis believes that the crucial first step in that transformation came when the staff began to honestly confront data on student achievement and to work together to improve results rather than make excuses for them.

Of course, this focus on continual improvement and results requires educators to change traditional practices and revise prevalent assumptions. Educators must begin to embrace data as a useful indicator of progress. They must stop disregarding or excusing unfavorable data and honestly confront the sometimes-brutal facts. They must stop using averages to analyze student performance and begin to focus on the success of each student.

Educators who focus on results must also stop limiting improvement goals to factors outside the classroom, such as student discipline and staff morale, and shift their attention to goals that focus on student learning. They must stop assessing their own effectiveness on the basis of how busy they are or how many new initiatives they have launched and begin instead to ask, "Have we made progress on the goals that are most important to us?" Educators must stop working in isolation and hoarding their ideas, materials, and strategies and begin to work together to meet the needs of all students.

Hard Work and Commitment

The professional learning community model is a powerful new way of working together that profoundly affects the practices of schooling. But initiating and sustaining the concept requires hard work. It requires the school staff to focus on learning rather than teaching, work collaboratively on matters related to learning, and hold itself accountable for the kind of results that fuel continual improvement.

When educators do the hard work necessary to implement these principles, their collective ability to help all students learn will rise. If they fail to demonstrate the discipline to initiate and sustain this work, then their school is unlikely to become more effective, even if those within it claim to be a professional learning community. The rise or fall of the professional learning community concept depends not on the merits of the concept itself, but on the most important element in the improvement of any school—the commitment and persistence of the educators within it.

Reference

Marzano, R. (2003). *What works in schools: Translating research into action.* Alexandria, VA: ASCD.

Douglas Reeves

A school committed to high levels of learning for all students must confront these questions: "What are the most essential skills and knowledge each student must acquire, and what is the standard they must achieve to demonstrate their proficiency?" No writer in America has been more effective in presenting a persuasive rationale for the ethical imperative of articulating standards of learning for all students than Dr. Douglas Reeves.

Dr. Reeves is founder and chairman of the Center for Performance Assessment, an international organization dedicated to improving student achievement and educational equity. He also serves as a faculty member for leadership programs sponsored by the Harvard Graduate School of Education. A prolific writer, Dr. Reeves has authored many articles and books, including *Assessing Educational Leaders: Evaluating Performance for Improved Individual and Organizational Results; Accountability for Learning: How Teachers and School Leaders Can Take Charge; The Leader's Guide to Standards: A Blueprint for Educational Excellence and Equity;* and the best-selling *Making Standards Work*, now in its third edition.

In this chapter, Dr. Reeves advances three main arguments and offers practical and constructive approaches to standards, assessment, and accountability. He contends that schools and school systems must translate standards into a set of rational, relevant, and above all *focused* expectations or "power standards"; those standards must be accompanied by frequent, common assessments in the classroom; and state and local accountability systems must include not only test scores, but explicit indicators of adult behavior. A common thread that runs through his work is the need for the collaborative culture of a professional learning community if educators are to meet the challenges they face.

Dr. Douglas Reeves is a frequent keynote speaker in the United States and abroad for education, government, and business organizations. He can be reached at dreeves@makingstandardswork.com.

Chapter 3

Putting It All Together: Standards, Assessment, and Accountability in Successful Professional Learning Communities

Douglas Reeves

In an astonishingly short period of time, the standards movement has swept the nation. While only a handful of states had adopted academic standards in the early 1990s, the use of standards is now a matter of federal law and all 50 states have adopted one version or another. Although the terminology surrounding standards varies widely, the notion that an educational system should have a coherent set of expectations about what students should know and be able to do is widely held in public and private schools throughout the world. As standards have become commonplace in the United States, forests have been cleared to publish the documents accompanying academic standards. Every textbook and curriculum document in the land claims to be "standards-based," as if such an imprimatur were the educational equivalent of a "Good Housekeeping Seal of Approval" of a bygone era. The cynics were certain that—along with Outcomes-Based Education, Behavioral Objectives, Mastery Learning, and a host of other reform ideas—standards would go the way of the dinosaur and eventually be of interest only to educational paleontologists of a future era. Standards advocates, on the other hand, were certain that the battle was won with the passage of the No Child Left Behind Act in 2001. Both sides were wrong. The one thing that can be said with certainty is this: Standards are not enough.

This chapter advances three arguments:

- First, standards in their present form are inadequate as a foundation for improved achievement and professional practices. Schools and school systems must translate standards into a set of rational, relevant, and above all *focused* expectations that I have labeled "power standards."

- Second, standards must be accompanied by frequent common assessments in the classroom. While the nation may be, according to the charges of many critics, over-tested, our students are actually under-assessed. This critical distinction lies at the heart of effective reform efforts.

- Third, state and local accountability systems must include not only test scores, but also explicit indicators of adult behavior such as teaching practices, curriculum, leadership, and other influences on student achievement.

These three arguments are as important for senior leaders and policymakers at the district, state, and national level as they are for classroom educators. Without the support of each of these three pillars—standards, assessment, and accountability—the roof of educational progress will sag, crack, and crumble. As the last decade has taught us, standards without assessment are fantasies. Assessments not linked to standards are prescriptions for frustration. Accountability systems that evaluate students without taking into account the actions of educators and leaders are as useful as the health club whose only piece of equipment is a scale.

The members of this health club weigh themselves diligently and frequently, but are oblivious to the relationship between those numbers and what a more thoughtfully constructed health program might include: diet, exercise, and careful attention to the individual medical needs of each person. When the health club only measures weight, no one knows if the apparently successful weight loss is the result of diet and exercise or anorexia and drug abuse. If the "score"—weight or test scores—is the only information that is relevant, neither the organization nor the individuals within it have the opportunity to make systematic improvements.

The framework of a professional learning community (Dufour, DuFour, Eaker, & Karhanek, 2004) is inextricably linked to the effective integration of standards, assessment, and accountability. The concept of professionals in community with one another flies in the face of the line guaranteed to garner applause at many gatherings: "Just leave me alone and let me teach!" Teaching has traditionally been a solitary enterprise, with idiosyncratic judgment and personal preference trumping external demands for consistency, fairness, and effectiveness. While few people would dine in a restaurant where the chef tells the city health department to "Just leave me alone and let me cook!" or place our medical care in the hands of a physician who resisted external accountability and standards of professional practice, we regularly place our children in classrooms where collaboration is not only absent, but also actively resisted. Recognizing that organizational culture and structure will influence behavior, the leaders of professional learning communities balance the desire for professional autonomy with the fundamental principles and values that drive collaboration and mutual accountability.

Power Standards: From Fantasy to Focus

While academic standards vary widely in their specificity and clarity, they almost all have one thing in common: there are too many of them (Marzano & Kendall, 1998). It is not uncommon to find standards and accompanying curriculum documents that specify 80 or more learning objectives for a single subject in a single grade. Only a few states have prioritized standards, thus leaving the majority of teachers with two options: curriculum by default or curriculum by design. The default option stems from the fantasy that if an expectation is approved by a state department of education and supported with three-ring binders created by a district curriculum department, then it will happen in the classroom.

The strength of one's belief in the standards fantasy is inversely proportional to the distance one is from the classroom. While many classroom teachers who face diverse learning needs and limited time know that rapid coverage of standards is not a substitute for student understanding, standards and curriculum designers at the district, state, or national levels continue to publish documents that are distinguished more by their girth than their effectiveness.

Curriculum by default is the result of the urgency with which we often act—we inevitably run out of time, energy, and patience by the end of the school year. Curriculum by design, however, reflects decisions made before the school year begins. Curriculum by default involves exasperation and resignation; curriculum by design involves prioritization and planning. Later in this chapter, we will consider how to use the concept of "power standards" to supplant curriculum by default with thoughtful design.

Standards: The Best Alternative to the Bell Curve

Unfortunately, the response of some people who have reasonable criticisms of bad standards is the unwarranted conclusion that state standards in general are flawed and should be discarded (Kohn, 1999; Ohanian, 1999). A better approach is to recognize that while standards are deeply flawed, they can and must be improved. If we fail to take such a constructive approach, then the inevitable result will be a return to the bell curve, a process of evaluating student achievement not based upon objective comparison of student performance to a standard, but by the pernicious and destructive process of evaluating student performance based upon who beat whom (Reeves, 2001b).

However flawed standards may be in their present form, they are vastly superior to the bell curve. The comparative approach to evaluation represented by the bell curve not only devastates underperforming students but also provides a sense of inappropriate complacency to the student who performs well relative to fellow students, but who nevertheless does not meet an objective standard. Every reader can think of a student who scored "above average" on a national norm-referenced literacy assessment, but who was unable to meet a state or local standard for writing and reading comprehension.

Criteria for Power Standards

The answer, therefore, is neither the continued proliferation of fantasy standards nor the rejection of all standards, but the establishment of power standards (Ainsworth, 2003; Reeves, 2000). In order to be identified as a power standard, an academic expectation (call them what you will—standards, objectives, curriculum elements, benchmarks) must meet three criteria:

1. Endurance

2. Leverage

3. Essential for the next level of instruction

First, it must have **endurance**, a characteristic of those standards whose importance lasts longer than a few nanoseconds after the termination of a state test. The principle of endurance is reflected in the recurring nature of key skills and knowledge that students must display. In some cases, enduring standards can be found in standards documents themselves. Reading comprehension, descriptive writing, and inferential reasoning can be found in academic standards from the early primary to the final secondary years. In other cases, however, the principle of endurance occurs in implicit standards, such as those involving time management, project management, and personal organization. While state academic content standards rarely consider these matters, every teacher who has considered the fate of a failing student knows the relative importance of academic content and time/project management, and those teachers will choose the latter as an enduring priority for student success.

Second, a power standard must have **leverage**. The principle of leverage means that success in one standard is very likely to be associated with success in other standards. The most notable application of the principle of leverage is the association between nonfiction writing, a power standard if ever there was one, and student success in math, social studies, and science (Calkins, 1994; Darling-Hammond, 1997; Reeves, 2000, 2001a, 2004a, 2004b). Another example of the principle of leverage is the mathematics standard requiring students to create and draw inferences from tables, charts, and graphs. This standard will not only lead to student success in mathematics, but will also help students record and interpret results from a science experiment and better analyze and understand data in economics, geography, history, health, and physical education courses.

The third criterion for power standards is that it **is essential for the next level of instruction**. When I ask audiences of educators what they are willing to give up from their curriculum, they are almost invariably silent, insisting that every element of their curriculum is vital, required by state standards, might be mentioned on a state test, and will be needed by their students in future years. But when I ask the same group to give advice to teachers in the next lower grade about what students must know and be able to do in order to advance to the next class with success and confidence, I have never—not a single time in thousands of cases—heard the words, "The teacher in the grade lower than me should cover every single standard." Rather, when giving advice to colleagues in a lower grade, educators are remarkably brief and balanced. They are able to give a list of a dozen or fewer critical educational, behavioral, and organizational needs that every student must meet. They routinely disregard the presumption that teacher coverage of every standard is a relevant part of the conversation.

The Role of Professional Learning Communities

While supposed respect is granted by various constituencies with the inclusion in the standards of a favorite court case, geographic feature, constitutional amendment, or historical event, real respect for these subjects is diluted by the constrictions of time and the imminence of state-mandated tests.

Standards, in sum, are a necessary but insufficient element of the equation for improving student achievement and educational equity. Without the articulation of standards, the evaluative scheme for students will inevitably revert to the bell curve, discouraging underperforming students and failing to challenge high-performing students. With only the articulation of standards, however, students and teachers are left with unprioritized curriculum chaos. Professional learning communities add value to standards not by merely delivering them to the schoolhouse door, but by also analyzing, synthesizing, and prioritizing them in a way that allows every teacher to wisely allocate time and instructional focus. Only when these steps have been taken can a school proceed to the second component necessary for excellence: assessment for learning.

Assessment for Learning: The Key to Continuous Improvement

Stiggins and associates (2000, 2004) and Wiggins (1998) thoughtfully distinguish between "assessment *of* learning" and "assessment *for* learning." While the former is designed merely to render a report, the latter is designed to actively engage students and teachers and improve their performance. With far less literary elegance, I have used the analogy of physicals and autopsies (Reeves, 2000, 2004a).

Without putting too fine a point on the metaphor, physicals at a certain point in life can be an uncomfortable ordeal but, on the whole, they are preferable to and less intrusive than autopsies. The wise physician does not use the annual physical only to evaluate the patient, but also to recommend improvements in lifestyle. From the best of our family doctors, we receive not the hieroglyphics of lab results, but also candid advice to replace candy with carrots and the television with a treadmill. The keys to assessment for learning—the physical rather than the autopsy—are consistency, timeliness, and differentiation.

Consistency in Assessment

As a teacher through and through, I cannot resist giving assignments, even when my students are readers on the other side of a printed page. I have learned that the best assignments are those that provide opportunities for discovery, challenge, and genuine "A-ha!" moments. Please consider the following assignment, as it will make the point more vividly than any external evidence or research analysis that I could otherwise provide.

1. Go to three different classrooms in the same grade that are studying the same subject and learning the same unit.

2. From each classroom, gather three pieces of student work that have received a grade of B or, if the teacher uses the language of standards, a grade of "proficient." This is not the best work or the worst, but clearly work that the teacher and students regard as acceptable. You now have nine pieces of student work, all of which purport to represent student success in the same subject, same grade, and same unit.

3. Cut off the name of the student, school, and teacher. Blot out any indicator of the grade on the paper. You are thus left with nine pieces of otherwise undifferentiated student work.

4. Copy these nine exhibits and distribute them at a faculty meeting, telling your colleagues only that these nine pieces of work are all from the same grade and represent student work on the same subject.

5. Ask the following penetrating questions: What do you think? What do you notice? You can expect to hear a cacophony of responses:

   • "What? I can't believe that this is fifth grade work! My students do better than this!"

   • "Check out sample #4—it's superior—are you sure that this student is in the right grade?"

   • "Somebody said that this work was okay? In my class, it would have flunked."

   • "This is exceptional! I'd love to have students who took an assignment this seriously."

   Listen patiently to the observations of your colleagues.

6. Write their observations of dramatic differences in the student work samples on chart paper that will be visible to everyone in the room.

7. When they have exhausted their analysis of profound differences in the nine samples of student work, deliver your punch line:

"Colleagues, I am confused. All nine of these samples of student work were in the same subject, the same grade, and the same unit. All nine of them received the same grade. Yet all I have heard from you are insightful observations about the profound differences in these work samples. I really trust the accuracy of your observations, so that must mean that our individual evaluation of student work is woefully inconsistent. If assessment of student work is so unclear to us as college-educated professionals, how unclear and confusing must it be to our students?"

Timeliness: The "Nintendo Effect"

If assessment feedback is to be effective, it is not enough that it is accurate and consistent. It must also be provided to the student in a timely manner (Marzano, Pickering, & Pollock, 2001). A compelling metaphor for timely assessment feedback is what Jeff Howard, founder of the Efficacy Institute, refers to as the "Nintendo Effect." Consider the distracted and inattentive student who, for reasons I cannot imagine, finds my middle school math class less than enthralling. This student appears to be constitutionally unable to sit still, focus, and concentrate. Before we reach for a pharmaceutical solution or, more commonly, give up on the student, perhaps we should observe the same student playing a Nintendo™ video game.

At the flip of a switch, the previously distracted and inattentive student is now silently focused like a laser and completely engaged. Even when he receives negative feedback (Nintendo players, after all, die at the conclusion of each game), he comes back for more, sometimes for hours at a time. What is Nintendo giving him that I am failing to provide in my math and writing classes? Feedback—but not just any feedback. Nintendo provides feedback that is specific, accurate, incremental, and timely. At the conclusion of every game, students have a very clear idea of what they did wrong and how to do better next time. How many students would play Nintendo if their scores were given to them days or weeks after playing the game? How many would play if they only received a score, but did not have a clear idea of how to improve their score? How many would play if they concluded that success at Nintendo was a function of skin color, language, or wealth? The cross-cultural success of Nintendo reminds us that timely feedback is effective for every single student. For the record, we might note that Nintendo provides the same accurate, incremental, and timely feedback to every student because Nintendo does not know the gender, ethnicity, or income level of the players. It just provides feedback that helps everyone improve.

I find the electronic game analogy troubling because, after all, school is much more important than a game, is it not? This is a good opportunity to ponder the seriousness that students and society in general give to games. Our society demands consistency and fairness in electronic games and all varieties of sports. Watch closely the next time a close call by athletic officials goes against your team. Failures in consistency result in screams from the sidelines from parents, teachers, and students, all united in common cause. They all are providing collective feedback that is, to say the least, specific and timely. Their demand for consistency and fairness is fueled by indignation and zeal. How I wish that the emotional energy invested in games was also invested in academic performance and assessment. If the game analogy borders on the offensive for some readers, there are many other examples of effective feedback models in schools.

My favorite is the music teacher. When the cellos are out of tune or the altos are off-key, the music teacher does not haul out the grade book to document a reason for a low grade weeks hence. Great music teachers stop, correct the problem, and then improve individual, small group, and large group performance. Students leave every class knowing that they are better than when then came in. Lucy Calkins (1983, 1994), founder of the Columbia University Literacy Project, helps teachers create an environment for providing immediate and meaningful feedback on student writing in much the same way that great music teachers generate continued enthusiasm from their students. Of one of her students, Professor Calkins (1983) wrote the following when a group of visitors observed the child's superior writing:

> "Susie is gifted," the visitors said, and I agreed. Gifted with the courage and the skills to experiment with writing. Gifted with the human potential to learn through trial and error.

The writing abilities of the children in this classroom were quite remarkable. Yet there had been nothing remarkable about their growth as writers. Susie's skills had not appeared full-blown out of nowhere nor had those of her classmates. Instead, the skills developed step-by-step, the way all learning happens. Susie's magic touch was not the result of a miracle but of experience and good teaching. She was not born with a talent for writing. She'd developed that talent through working at her craft. She'd gained a skill through the process of doing her best and then making her best better. (p. 88)

Differentiation

The clarion call for consistency in previous paragraphs seems at first to fly in the face of the suggestion that effective assessments must be differentiated. Indeed, there are many people who have used the label of "differentiation" to justify terrible professional practices and low expectations. Effective differentiation in assessment does not dilute academic standards or rigorous expectations. Rather, differentiated assessment acknowledges that students must be able to show what they know in a variety of different ways. While some students can demonstrate proficiency using traditional multiple choice tests, others will demonstrate similar or higher levels of proficiency when they write, demonstrate, or otherwise engage in performances that display their knowledge and skills. The use of standards-based performance assessments is, in fact, more rigorous than the typical multiple-choice test (Reeves, 2002).

Teachers who want to more fully engage students in daily work, tests, and projects will find that they can maintain higher levels of student energy and commitment if they combine a consistently high level of academic rigor and expectations with a variety of alternative assessments. Rather than assuming that every student needs the same level of skill development, teachers create homework menus, engage the interest of students who might be bored by typical homework assignments, and help develop fundamental skills in students who came to the class without adequate preparation. Tests and projects can provide consistent levels of rigor and standards, while also providing a variety of alternative methods for demonstrating knowledge. An excellent way for students to demonstrate the depth of their understanding of a subject is for them to create their own test questions and write their own scoring rubrics (Ainsworth & Christinson, 1998), creating an optimal combination of engagement, rigor, and differentiation.

In the hands of a capable professional learning community, assessment is relentlessly constructive and focused on its singular purpose—the improvement of teaching and learning. Classroom assessments reflect consistently high expectations while providing a rich variety of methods for meeting a complex array of student needs. The feedback from these assessments is consistent—one teacher's "proficiency" is not another teacher's "superior"—and the communication of this feedback is timely. In the final section of this chapter, we will consider how to take the lessons of effective assessment and apply them to educational accountability systems involving many schools.

Accountability: The Leadership and Learning Connection

Even the best standards and assessments will undermine student learning if professional practices are subverted by counterproductive accountability systems. Despite pervasive complaints that accountability policies of federal and state governments dominate school decision-making, there is a growing body of evidence that accountability can be constructive, comprehensive, and supportive of professional learning and student achievement (Reeves, 2000, 2004a; Schmoker, 2001). Effective accountability systems are not merely a litany of test scores; they also include three critical levels of information:

- **Tier 1** indicators reflect typical accountability data, including test scores and other data required for external accountability. But if we stopped there, as too many schools do, we would not understand the causes of improved achievement. It would be as if we knew an obese student had lost weight, but we did not know if the causes were diet and exercise or anorexia and drug abuse. That is why effective school accountability systems include Tier 2 data.

- **Tier 2** data are made up of measurable indicators that reflect professional practices in teaching, curriculum, and leadership.

- **Tier 3** of this accountability system is a school narrative, allowing teachers and school leaders to provide a qualitative context for quantitative data—the story behind the numbers.

Only with this system will accountability systems provide the appropriate context, allowing professional learning communities to explore both the causes and effects surrounding improved student performance and professional practices.

Refined and Focused Standards

The three pillars of standards, assessment, and accountability support the effectiveness of professional learning communities. Remove one of those pillars and the structure will sag, crack, and eventually break. Standards must not merely be delivered from the state department to the schoolhouse door; they must be refined and focused. Assessment must not be the subject of annual academic post-mortems, but the focus of continuous discussion by professionals throughout the year. Accountability systems must focus not only on what students achieve, but also on how the adults in the system influenced that achievement.

References

Ainsworth, L. (2003). *Power standards: Identifying the standards that matter most.* Englewood, CO: Advanced Learning Press.

Ainsworth, L., & Christinson, J. (1998). *Student-generated rubrics: An assessment model to help all students succeed.* Assessment Bookshelf Series. Orangeburg, NY: Dale Seymour Publications.

Calkins, L. M. (1983). *Lessons from a child: On the teaching and learning of writing.* Portsmouth, NH: Heinemann.

Calkins, L. M. (1994). *The art of teaching writing.* Portsmouth, NH: Heinemann.

Darling-Hammond, L. (1997). *The right to learn: A blueprint for creating schools that work.* San Francisco: Jossey-Bass.

DuFour, R. (2002). The learning-centered principal. *Educational Leadership, 59*(8), 12–15.

DuFour, R., DuFour, R., Eaker, R., & Karhanek, G. (2004). *Whatever it takes: How professional learning communities respond when kids don't learn.* Bloomington, IN: Solution Tree (formerly National Educational Service).

Kohn, A. (1999). *The schools our children deserve: Moving beyond traditional classrooms and "tougher standards."* NY: Houghton Mifflin.

Marzano, R. J., & Kendall, J. S. (1998). *Implementing standards-based education (student assessment series).* Washington, DC: National Educational Association.

Marzano, R. J., Pickering, D. J., & Pollock, J. E. (2001). *Classroom instruction that works. Research-based strategies for increasing student achievement.* Alexandria, VA: Association for Supervision and Curriculum Development.

Ohanian, S. (1999). *One size fits few: The folly of educational standards.* Portsmouth, NH: Heinemann.

Reeves, D. B. (2000). *Accountability in action: A blueprint for learning organizations.* Denver: Advanced Learning Press.

Reeves, D. B. (2001a). *101 questions & answers about standards, assessment, and accountability.* Denver: Advanced Learning Press.

Reeves, D. B. (2001b, June 6). If you hate standards, learn to love the bell curve. *Education Week,* p. 48.

Reeves, D. B. (2002). *Making standards work: How to implement standards-based performance assessments in the classroom, school, and district* (3rd ed.). Denver: Advanced Learning Press.

Reeves, D. B. (2004a). *Accountability for learning: How teachers and school leaders can take charge.* Alexandria, VA: Association for Supervision and Curriculum Development.

Reeves, D. B. (2004b). *101 more questions & answers about standards, assessment, and accountability.* Denver: Advanced Learning Press.

Schmoker, M. (2001). *The results fieldbook: Practical strategies from dramatically improved schools.* Alexandria, VA: Association for Supervision and Curriculum Development.

Stiggins, R. J. (2000). *Student-involved classroom assessment* (3rd ed.). Upper Saddle River, NJ: Prentice Hall.

Stiggins, R. J., Arter, J., Chappuis, J., & Chappuis, S. (2004). *Classroom assessment for student learning: Doing it right, using it well.* Portland, OR: Assessment Training Institute.

Wiggins, G. (1998). *Educative assessment: Designing assessments to inform and improve student performance.* San Francisco: Jossey-Bass.

Rick Stiggins

One of the critical questions that drives the work of teams in a professional learning community is "How will we know when each child has mastered the essential knowledge and skills we have determined all students must acquire?" Dr. Rick Stiggins, one of the nation's foremost authorities on assessment, created the Assessment Training Institute (ATI) in 1992 to assist educators in answering that question. Under his direction, ATI has become a leading force in school improvement.

Dr. Stiggins has served as an assessment director for a school district, director of test development for the American College Testing Program, and director of the Center for Classroom Assessment at the Northwest Regional Educational Laboratory. He is the author of several books and videos, including the award-winning *Student-Involved Classroom Assessment*.

In this chapter, Dr. Stiggins argues that schools have traditionally used assessments to sort and select students—to create winners and losers by the end of school. He asserts that if educators are to achieve "learning for all," they must use assessment in very different ways. He contends that carefully-developed assessments *for* learning, when done well, can inform teacher/team practice, help students assess and manage their own growth toward clearly articulated and relevant standards, and promote and encourage learning. He prescribes student-involved assessment *for* learning as a central element in any school that hopes to function as a PLC.

Dr. Stiggins provides a five-step plan for teams to follow as they implement student-involved formative assessment to support learning in conjunction with periodic common assessments *of* learning to ensure accountability. He calls upon educators to replace teacher isolation with cooperation and collaboration and to replace student anxiety and competition with strategies that encourage their confidence as learners.

For more information about Dr. Rick Stiggins and his work, visit www.assessmentinst.com, call 800-480-3060, or contact Solution Tree at 800-733-6786.

Chapter 4

Assessment FOR Learning: Building a Culture of Confident Learners*

Rick Stiggins

In education, we assess for two reasons: (1) to gather evidence of student achievement to inform instructional decisions and (2) to motivate learning. Virtually all school improvement models contend that schools will become more effective if the right people have access to the right evidence analyzed in the right way and used to inform the right decisions. The dominant view of what constitutes the right evidence is that if we develop the right kinds of standardized tests and analyze the results in the right manner, then the path to productive learning environments will reveal itself. Over the past 6 decades, we have progressed from district-wide standardized testing to state-wide testing to national and finally to international testing in search of the right evidence.

---

*Copyright © 2004, Assessment Training Institute, Portland, Oregon. Adapted and published by permission.

However, research suggests that this dominant view has been shortsighted. Even with the billions of dollars spent over 60 years on the multiple levels of standardized testing noted previously, there is scant evidence that schools have become more effective. Leaders in the field of assessment testify to this:

> As someone who has spent his entire career doing research, writing, and thinking about educational testing and assessment issues, I would like to conclude by summarizing a compelling case showing that the major uses of tests for student and school accountability during the past 50 years have improved education and student learning in dramatic ways. Unfortunately, that is not my conclusion. (Linn, 2000, p. 14)

In fact, Amrein and Berliner (2002), as well as Harlen and Crick (2003), summarize evidence that the motivation and achievement of some students actually suffer as a result of high-stakes standardized testing.

In this chapter, I explore why this is so. In doing so, my agenda is not to advocate for the abandonment of our traditional standardized testing. To be sure, the effective use of test results by carefully trained school leaders to inform their important programmatic and policy-level decisions can represent a critical ingredient in our school improvement equation under certain conditions. I will argue that those conditions have never been satisfied and so this potential has never been realized.

More importantly, our view of assessment as test scores that merely *index* the effects of school improvement efforts has been so dominant that it has prevented us from understanding how to use assessment as a process that can *cause*

increased student learning. For example, we could have been using day-to-day classroom assessment as instruction in ways, evidence shows, that greatly enhance student learning, thus making periodic standardized test scores rise sharply and continuously over the long haul.

Extensive research evidence gathered around the world consistently reveals effect sizes (gains in standardized test scores) of a half to a full standard deviation and more directly attributable to the effective use of classroom assessment to support student learning (Black & Wiliam, 1998; Bloom, 1984; Meisels, Atkins-Burnett, Xue, Bickel, & Son, 2003; and Rodriguez, 2004). This research reveals that such gains occur when we:

- Share clear and appropriate learning targets with students from the beginning of the learning.

- Increase the accuracy of classroom assessments of those targets.

- Make sure that students have continuous access to descriptive feedback.

- Involve students continuously in classroom assessment, record keeping, and communication processes.

Thus, it becomes clear that accurate student-involved classroom assessment practices represent critically important components of effective instruction and, therefore, should occupy a very prominent place in the growth plans of any professional learning community.

In the chapter that follows, I will explore why these practices work so well. It is because they constantly leave learners in an emotional state that predisposes them to act productively on assessment results. In short, in our zeal to use assessment to inform instructional decisions, I will argue, we have failed to tap productive uses of assessment for the second purpose listed in my opening paragraph: to motivate learning.

Assessment as a Motivational Trigger

In addition to using assessment to inform decisions, it also has been our tradition to use assessment—the pending final exam, the unanticipated pop quiz—as the primary trigger for student motivation. To maximize learning, our teachers believed you had to maximize anxiety. And assessment was always the great intimidator.

In a similar sense, the accountability movement that has become so much a part of the school improvement process since the 1960s also is intended to trigger motivation among school leaders, teachers, and students alike, all of whom might be labeled "failures." Society has "raised the bar" to "world-class standards" transformed into "high-stakes tests," with dire consequences attached to low scores, to drive motivation and effort. Pressure to raise test scores, society believes, will increase motivation and yield more effective schools.

However, because of a recent change in the mission that society has assigned to its schools, the emotions triggered by assessment in the past that have been regarded as *productive* now reveal themselves to be *counterproductive*. To see why, we must look back and examine our assessment legacy and its effects. Then we can use this as a point of departure from which to anticipate what might be possible in the future.

The Old Mission and Its Emotional Legacy

We grew up in schools assigned the mission of ranking us from the highest to the lowest achiever by the end of high school. The role of our schools was to help sort or channel us into the various segments of our social and economic system. The amount of time available to learn was fixed: 1 year per grade. The amount learned by the end of that time varied: some learned a lot, some very little. Thirteen years of such treatment and those who remained in school were, in effect, spread along an achievement continuum and were assigned a rank in class. If the rank order was dependable, schools were deemed by the community to have worked effectively.

From the very beginning of this process, starting in the earliest grades, some students learned a great deal very quickly and scored consistently high on tests. The emotional effect of this was to help them come to see themselves as capable learners—they became increasingly confident in school. That confidence gave them the inner emotional strength to take the risk of striving for more success, because they believed success was within reach if they tried. Driven forward by their optimism, they continued to try hard and that continued to result in success for them. They became the academic and emotional winners. The trigger for their emotions was assessment success.

But at the same time, there were other students who learned more slowly for a variety of reasons, and thus scored very low on tests even in the earliest grades. The emotional effect in this case was to cause them to question their own capabilities as learners. They began to lose confidence, which, in turn, deprived them of the emotional reserves to continue to risk trying. Public failure was embarrassing—it simply hurt too much to continue. Better not to try and save face. As their motivation waned, of course, their performance plummeted. They entered what they believed to be an irreversible tumble of inevitable failure and thus became the academic and emotional losers. The trigger was their performance on assessments.

In this environment, if some students lost hope and gave up in hopelessness, this was not a problem because such emotions served the mission of schools: expand the spread of achievement. The broader the range of differences among students, the more dependable the rank order would be. Thus, if some students gave up and stopped trying (even dropped out of school), that was regarded as their problem, not the school's.

This system represented a concrete manifestation of the strong societal belief that the way to maximize student learning is through behavior management: reward success at learning and the behavior that seems to lead to it and we maximize achievement; punish low achievement and the behavior that seems to lead to it and students either straighten out or give up.

Within this set of beliefs, we find the psychological foundations of the traditional report card grading systems used in schools. High grades are seen as rewards. These are thought to build confidence, promote strong effort, and yield more success. Low grades are intimidating, punishing, and, if perpetual, defeating. Winners and losers were exactly what society felt it needed and wanted from its schools: a dependable rank order by the end of high school.

Grades became the monetary system used to trigger what were believed to be the proper emotions associated with learning. However, since everything counted toward the grade, there was no time to practice without risk—no time for the low performer to recover and to become successful. Attention (adulation, even) and resources were showered on those who succeeded at assessment time. The unsuccessful were accommodated unless they gave up in hopelessness and left. In any event, failure was the student's problem to deal with—not the teacher's or school's.

And, to be sure, the impact of these assessment-related emotions on student behavior and learning did not stop there. Often, they led students to the belief that it was in their best interest to misrepresent the truth about their own achievement. The anxiety associated with the possibility of failure and relatively low standing in the rank order has been the trigger for cheating at assessment time. In the schools that I attended, if we failed to understand or learn something for any reason, it was distinctly dangerous for us to admit this, because honesty about such matters could only lead to lower grades. It was better to cheat and risk getting caught if we had not learned the material because the effect of taking the test honestly or getting caught cheating would be the same—failure. We had nothing to lose. There was always the chance that we might get away with it.

Notice how little any of this has to do with real learning and academic success. Notice how it seems to doom some students to the inevitable failure in which schools intentionally leave a lot of students behind.

Also notice who is making the "data-based instructional decisions": not teachers, not school leaders, not policy makers—rather, it is students themselves. They are deciding whether success is within or beyond reach, whether the learning is worth the effort, and therefore, whether to try or give up. For many, the critical emotions underpinning the decision-making process include anxiety, fear of failure, uncertainty, willingness to risk trying or not, and honesty or dishonesty—all triggered by assessment results. Who is not troubled at least occasionally by that dream in which the final exam is at hand and we have not been studying or even going to class? Guilt and vulnerability are the gifts that keep on giving.

Some students responded to the demands of such learning environments by working hard and learning a great deal in order to keep the anxiety at bay. Others controlled their own anxiety by giving up in hopelessness and not caring. The result was that these practices drove down the achievement of many students. And the evidence is that the victims in this case were and are more frequently members of particular socioeconomic and ethnic minorities.

A New Mission and Its Emotional Promise

Recently, however, society has come to understand the extreme limitations of schools that merely rank students. We have discovered that the bottom third to half of the student population, plus all who drop out before being ranked, fail to develop the foundational reading, writing, and math problem-solving proficiencies needed to survive in, let alone contribute to, an increasingly complex culture. So now society is asking schools to raise the floor of the rank order up to a certain level of minimum competence. We call those expectations our "academic achievement standards." Every state has them and schools are being held accountable for *helping all students* meet them.

To be clear, the mission of sorting has not been removed. For the foreseeable future, students will be ranked at the end of high school. However, society now dictates that the celebration of differences in amount learned must start at a certain level of achievement for all.

The implications of this change in mission for the role of assessment are profound. Now assessment and grading procedures designed to permit only a few students to succeed (those at the top of the rank order distribution) must be revised to permit all students to succeed at some appropriate level. Further, procedures that permitted (perhaps even encouraged) some students to give up in hopelessness and stop trying now must be replaced by those that promote hope and continuous effort for all. In short, the entire emotional environment surrounding the prospect of being evaluated must change, especially for perennial low achievers.

The student's mission is no longer merely to beat the others. Each must come to understand that at least part of his or her goal is to become competent. The teachers must actually believe that all students can achieve a certain level of academic success, because those teachers must help all of their students believe this, too. Teachers must understand that students learn at different rates and not merely use that fact as the basis for a dependable rank. Rather, learning environments must accommodate differences in learning rate by allowing some students more time to learn. This requires that we ensure that all students believe that success is within reach if they keep trying.

The driving emotional force cannot merely be competition for an artificial scarcity of success. Because all can and must succeed at some level, cooperation and collaboration must come into play. The driving emotional forces must be confidence and optimism. The student must believe that, "I will succeed at learning if I keep trying." Students must have continuous access to believable evidence of credible academic success, leading to the new role for assessment in school improvement: We use it to help students see and understand the achievement target from the very beginning of the learning, and we use it to help them watch themselves grow and then succeed.

In our work at the Assessment Training Institute, we call this *assessment FOR learning* (Stiggins, Arter, Chappuis, & Chappuis, 2005), a concept that heralds a fundamentally different vision of the relationship between assessment and the emotions of student success. Under the old mission, only the few who succeeded became increasingly confident, assertive, risk-taking learners. With assessment FOR learning, all students can experience the joy that arises from these emotions. In this way, no child is left behind.

Differentiating Assessment OF and FOR Learning

Our assessment legacy has been to use assessment to check achievement status. Traditionally, we have used assessments to discover how much our students have learned up to a particular point in time. Our habit of mind has been to feed those results to the adults in the system, as outlined above, so they can make informed instructional decisions to help students. This certainly makes sense in terms of school improvement under certain conditions. But again, as argued above, such assessment OF learning, by itself, has not done the job. It is not that it has been inappropriate; it has been insufficient.

So let us supplement it with assessment FOR learning. Here we ask, "How can we use the assessment process not merely to gauge student learning, but also to cause students to learn more—that is, to increase achievement?" To accomplish this, we use assessment to inform students about themselves.

Further, if assessments OF learning ask if students are meeting standards (state, district, or classroom), assessments FOR learning ask if our students are making progress toward meeting those standards (day to day in the classroom). One is for accountability, while the other is intended to support learning. Both are important, but they are different because they serve fundamentally different purposes.

The key to our collective success as educators is to balance the two—to find the synergy between them. This is something that our old mission did not value. But our new mission of student competence must value it. For this reason, let me continue to differentiate between them so we can discover how to use them in harmony.

Examples of assessments OF learning arise from our legacy: externally imposed standardized tests like college admissions tests, state assessments, district-wide tests, and so on. But in addition, we must include classroom assessments used to assign report card grades such as unit tests, final exams, and the like. These all are assessments conducted after instruction has occurred to determine if learning has occurred. They inform multiple levels of accountability and important instructional decisions and, therefore, are critical.

Examples of assessments FOR learning are those that we use to diagnose student needs, merely for practice, or to help students watch themselves improve over time. In all cases, we seek to provide teachers and students with the kinds of information they need to make decisions that promote continued learning. Assessments FOR learning occur throughout the learning process while the learning is happening. So early in the learning, students' scores will not be high. This is not failure—it simply represents where students are now in their ongoing journey to ultimate success.

If assessment OF learning measures a student's mastery of standards, assessment FOR learning continuously tracks where that student is at any point in time on the scaffolding leading up to those standards. They are intended to provide that information both to student and teacher.

The teacher's role in assessment OF learning is as it always has been. If the standardized test is externally imposed, teachers follow prescribed test administration procedures and then use the scores as appropriate to enhance learning. If the assessment is an internal one for grading purposes, teachers develop an accurate assessment, administer it fairly, and follow sound procedures in determining the grade.

But in assessment FOR learning, this role changes. The teacher's role is to complete the following progression:

1. Start by clearly understanding the standard to be mastered.

2. Deconstruct it into the enabling classroom achievement targets that form the foundations of learning leading up to the standard.

3. Create a student-friendly version of those targets to share with students from the beginning of the learning.

4. Create high-quality assessments of those classroom targets.

5. Use those assessments in collaboration with students to track improvement over time.

The student's role in assessment OF learning is as it always has been: study hard and strive for the highest score. But in assessment FOR learning contexts, that role changes. The student's role is not necessarily to strive to get a high score or grade. Rather it is to strive to understand what success looks like and to use each assessment to try to understand how to do better the next time. Everything centers on getting better over time with the student as a key player in the ongoing assessment and record-keeping processes.

This leads to a fundamental redefinition of the relationship between assessment and student motivation. Rather than relying on assessment as the source of information used to decide who is rewarded and punished, we use assessment as a road map from start to ultimate success. Success at learning becomes its own reward, promoting confidence and persistence.

Both assessments OF and FOR learning are important because they serve important purposes. But those purposes (users and uses) are different. We tap the full potential of assessment as a school improvement tool when we find the synergy between the two, when we find ways to make them work in harmony with each other in the service of student success. Our aspiration should be to create learning environments characterized by a continuous array of classroom assessments FOR learning punctuated by periodic classroom and standardized assessments OF learning. Assessment promotes growth and then verifies it.

To make this work, both assessments OF and FOR learning must arise from exactly the same academic achievement standards, but they will treat those standards differently. The former asks if students have met the standards, while the latter asks if students are making progress on their journey toward meeting the standards. Both assessments OF and FOR learning must collect and use accurate information about student achievement; both must rely on high-quality assessments. Results from both must be given to the intended user in a timely and understandable form. That is, effective communication is essential. We will address these matters of accuracy and effective information management in later sections of this chapter.

Assessment FOR Learning: The Trigger for Productive Emotions

Teachers have various specific interventions available to them to bring students into the classroom assessment process:

- Student self-assessment

- Student-involved record keeping

- Student-involved communication about their achievement success

Early in the learning process, we might engage our students as partners in the creation of practice versions of assessments like those that they will be held accountable for at some point in the future. We do this to reveal to them what success will look like when they achieve it. In addition, we do it to reveal to them where they are now in relation to success so that the path to success becomes clear to them. This is the confidence builder, the source of optimism, the energizer. We want students to say, "I am not there yet, but I know where 'there' is, and I'm on my way."

Then, as students travel the journey toward success over time, if we engage them in repeated self-assessments with standards of excellence held constant, they begin to see and feel in control of the gains in their own capabilities. We might, for example, have them build growth portfolios—not for account-ability or grading, but to reflect continuously on their own improvement. This is another confidence builder. We help them say, "I am not there yet, but I am much closer than I was and, if I keep trying, I am going to get there."

As they make progress and hopefully arrive at success, we then provide them with the opportunity to tell the story of their journey by presenting their evidence of improvement to classmates, their teachers, or in student-led parent teacher con-ferences. By doing so, we tap a wellspring of productive emo-tions that reside within each learner that we simply cannot tap merely by threatening Fs and promising As. If done well, this practice triggers a deep internal shift in the student's sense of responsibility for her or his own success and a pride in accom-plishment that forms an emotional foundation for success.

The Necessary Conditions

Four specific conditions must be satisfied in the classroom to tap the power of assessment FOR learning.

Teachers must understand and be prepared to satisfy the information needs of student decision makers. They must know and understand the specific instructional decisions that students make (and that teachers want them to make correctly) on their journey to academic success. Students and teachers must work in harmony as assessment users to promote maximum student confidence, motivation, and achievement.

Achievement expectations must be clear and appropriate. State and local achievement standards must be articulated and decon-structed into the enabling classroom achievement targets that form the scaffolding upon which students will climb on their journey to meet those standards. Further, teachers must be competent and confident masters of the achievement targets their students are expected to reach. Only then can they share student-friendly versions of those targets from the beginning of the learning and in ways that help students watch themselves grow.

Classroom assessments must be accurate. They must feed dependable information into the mutual decision-making process. This means they must:

- Rely on proper assessment methods that take into account the target to be measured

- Include high-quality test items or performance tasks accompanied by sound scoring procedures

- Provide enough evidence to lead to a proper conclusion about student achievement

- Be designed and used in a manner that prevents bias from creeping in and distorting results

During the learning, students must be partners in the creation and use of assessments in ways that keep them in touch with the ultimate target and their proximity to it.

Communication systems must deliver assessment results into the hands of their intended users (including students) in a timely and understandable manner. The focus must be on providing the descriptive feedback needed to help students understand how to do better the next time. That feedback must be sharply focused and provided in doses learners can deal with productively (that is, not so much as to overwhelm or so little as to be trivial). Principles of effective communication must be adhered to:

- Those involved in gathering and delivering results and those receiving the results must both hold the same vision of successful achievement.

- The evidence must be accurate (as described in the third condition).

- The symbols used to convey information (such as grades, scores, and so on) must carry the same meaning for all involved.

- The receiver of results must be open to hearing and acting on those results.

In addition, all of this must function effectively in an environment in which students trust that it is safe to risk trying. They need to believe that their teacher is patient and is willing and able to grant them time to progress to the agreed-upon standard. They must trust that they can play a role in setting goals for their own learning. They must know that they can be responsible for providing the evidence to show they are succeeding. Students need to trust each other as valuable allies to turn to, as appropriate, for insight on how to enhance the quality of their work.

In the same sense, teachers must truly believe that all students can learn when given the time and support needed to do so. They must understand that not all students will grow at the same rate and be willing to build learning environments that accommodate those differences.

Building a Community of Confidence Through Assessment

These are the features of classroom assessment climates geared to instill confidence in learners. That confidence triggers optimism, or the expectation of a positive result in the future. That expectation, in turn, triggers the desire and energy needed to strive for success with gusto. The result will be a culture of confidence and profound gains in student learning.

A professional learning community can provide an excellent environment within which to develop such a culture. The Assessment Training Institute has created a professional development program that permits teachers and school leaders to join as learning teams to develop their mastery of sound classroom assessment practices. I believe that this type of team-based strategy for supporting adult learners represents the future of professional development. The workshop format for professional growth has not permitted us to learn through the application of and experimentation with new assessment practices *in real classrooms*. While workshops can build awareness, they do not permit the kind of collaborative interaction among colleagues that permits all to benefit from the insights of others. ATI learning teams overcome these limitations. Please refer to our web site, www.assessmentinst.com, or call us at 800-480-3060 for details.

In addition, as a result of this teamwork-based learning experience, teachers can continue to collaborate in the development and use of both assessments OF and FOR learning. To the extent that we team to (1) analyze, understand, and deconstruct standards, (2) transform them into high-quality classroom assessments, and (3) share and interpret results together, we benefit from the union of our wisdom about how to help our students continue to grow as learners. Just be cautious and understand that common assessments OF learning may not constitute assessments FOR learning if they do not satisfy the conditions of student involvement spelled out here. And we must always remain open to the possibility that assessments FOR learning may be unique to a single classroom or even to a single student—and are therefore not always "common." But to the extent that teachers can work together to meet the challenges of classroom assessment, we bring the power of the professional learning community into play to benefit students.

References

Amrein, A. L., & Berliner, D. C. (2002). High-stakes testing, uncertainty, and student learning. *Educational Policy Analysis Archives, 10*(18). Retrieved December 9, 2004, from http://epaa.asu.edu/epaa/v10n18/

Black, P., & Wiliam, D. (1998). Assessment and classroom learning. *Educational Assessment: Principles, Policy and Practice, 5*(1), 7–74.

Bloom, B. (1984). The search for methods of group instruction as effective as one-to-one tutoring. *Educational Leadership, 41*(8), 4–17.

Harlen, W., & Crick, R. D. (2003). Testing and motivation for learning. *Assessment in Education, 10,* 169–207.

Linn, R. (2000). Assessment and accountability. *Educational Researcher, 29*(2), 4–14.

Meisels, S., Atkins-Burnett, S., Xue, Y., Bickel, D. D., & Son, S.-H. (2003). Creating a system of accountability: The impact of instructional assessment on elementary children's achievement scores. *Educational Policy Analysis Archives, 11*(9). Retrieved December 9, 2004, from http://epaa.asu.edu/epaa/v11n9/

Rodriguez, M. C. (2004). The role of classroom assessment in student performance on TIMSS. *Applied Measurement in Education, 17*(1), 1–24.

Stiggins, R. J., Arter, J., Chappuis, J., & Chappuis, S. (2005). *Classroom assessment FOR student learning: Doing it right—Using it well.* Portland, OR: Assessment Training Institute.

Jonathon Saphier

Dr. Jonathon Saphier is one of North America's leading authorities on effective teaching and creating school cultures that promote effective teaching. He is the founder and chairman emeritus of Teachers 21, a nonprofit corporation focusing on public policy for the professionalization of teaching and comprehensive school improvement. Dr. Saphier is also the founder and president of Research for Better Teaching (RBT), established in 1979 to build teacher, leader, and institutional capacity to promote and sustain increased student learning and achievement. RBT calls for the creation of professional learning communities that believe in continual improvement and engage in the study of teaching and learning. He is the author of numerous professional articles and eight books including *The Skillful Teacher* (now in its 5th edition), *How to Bring Vision to School Improvement,* and *How to Make Decisions That Stay Made.*

In this chapter, Dr. Saphier explores the behavior of teachers and schools who have a belief in "effort-based ability": the belief that all children can do rigorous academic work even if they come to school needing a significant amount of time and support to catch up. He contends that this belief is especially critical in schools where the majority of students may start out several grade levels behind. He writes that this belief:

> ". . . makes a huge difference in how well staff members use the collaborative structures we create on behalf of student learning. It provides the energy needed to persevere when the work of schools is tough."

Dr. Saphier offers specific practices and language teachers can use with students and leaders can use with staff to strengthen their belief in effort-based ability. He challenges educators to create professional learning communities where the day-to-day actions of the adults and students create a school culture in which this transforming belief comes to life.

For more information on Dr. Jonathon Saphier, go to www.rbteach.com or contact Research for Better Teaching, Inc., at (978) 263-9449.

Chapter 5

Masters of Motivation

Jonathon Saphier

Many of the authors who have written chapters in this book are on record here and elsewhere as advocates of rigorous and authentic teacher "joint work": teachers working collaboratively in groups that have clear goals for student performance, that continuously examine real student results, and that look equally hard at their teaching to adjust it in light of student needs. However, there is another vital aspect of a professional learning community in addition to this well-structured teacher collaboration: the key beliefs of educators and the way those beliefs are manifested in individual behavior and school policies.

I am in the schools of our major cities each week working with teachers and principals. Sometimes I come home full of anger and sadness because I see dying spirits and hopeless suffering in the eyes of sweet first graders or in the faces of older children who alternate between swagger and despair—children who have no one to believe in them and convince them that they are able and worthwhile. But I also find myself in places that are uplifting because of what educators are accomplishing for their students. These places convey hope to all students about the promise of education and the capacity of each of them to *develop* their abilities.

In this essay, I will examine the behavior of teachers and schools in these uplifting places for a particular belief—"effort-based ability." This is the belief that all students can do rigorous academic work at high standards, even if they are far behind academically and need a significant amount of time to catch up. Educators who carry this belief into their practice are not unrealistic about the obstacles they and their students face. They simply have not given up. And we know for sure that they will get results if they translate this belief into appropriate practice.

Belief in effort-based ability makes a huge difference in how well staff members use the collaborative structures we create on behalf of student learning. It provides the energy and motivation needed to persevere when the work of schools is tough. In schools where the majority of students may start out several grade levels behind, it can be tough, indeed.

In the first part of this chapter, I will show how effort-based ability emerges in individual teacher behavior and in school-wide structures. In the second part, I will examine how leaders can influence and strengthen this belief in their staff members. This chapter has numerous references to schools for disadvantaged students. The strategies and structures of believing in effort-based ability are important for all schools, but they are essential if we want progress for schools serving disadvantaged children.

Crucial Messages for Effort-Based Ability

Let us start with a visit to a high-performing inner-city secondary school. We could visit any one of a dozen such schools where the students are chosen by lottery, there are no budgetary supplements, parent participation is erratic, and yet every senior is admitted to college. In this school almost all of the staff members would tell you some version of the following message:

> I believe that all of my students have the intellectual ability to do rigorous work and meet high standards. Unfortunately, not all of my students share this belief. It is my job to help them come to believe this, along with the conviction that it would be worth their while to do well in school. Therefore, in our minute-to-minute interactions, I communicate to students in every way I can the messages:
>
> 1. "This is important."
>
> 2. "You can do it."
>
> 3. "I won't give up on you."

Schools in which disadvantaged children who are far behind academically eventually succeed send these crucial messages through a variety of means, including:

- Interactive teaching behaviors

- Classroom structures and procedures

- Classroom climate and personal relationship building

- Explicit teaching of effective effort to all students

- School-wide structures for building a culture of aspiration, effective effort, and responsibility

- A focus on the future

Part One—"Putting Effort-Based Ability to Work"—examines each of these six structures and details specific strategies within each structure that teachers can use to promote the belief in effort-based ability in their students.

Masters of Motivation

Have you ever had someone in your life who consistently communicated to you that you were an able person, that you were valuable, and that you had worthwhile things to accomplish? Readers who have risen from humble circumstances almost always say "Yes!" and have a particular person in mind. Readers who come from affluent backgrounds may have a harder time identifying a single individual, but that may be because their whole culture and environment sent those messages. Teachers who send these messages and schools that are organized to do so get results that others do not.

The teachers in these successful schools are masters of motivation. The staff's willingness to work as hard as they do to learn and implement strategies in the six structures mentioned previously comes from their fundamental belief in student potential—all students' potential. These schools are led by committed and determined people, but they are not supermen and superwomen, nor do they rely on charisma. They are willing to work very hard and they bring significant expertise to that work.

Believing that all students have innate capacity and that academic ability can be grown is a *definitional element* of professional learning communities. Newmann and Wehlage (1995) call it "academic press." This commitment and determination are what lies behind the success of the strategies and structures that DuFour, DuFour, Eaker, and Karhanek (2004)

write about in *Whatever It Takes*. Effort-based ability might be less visible in the PLCs of affluent communities, though many children in these communities would have different school experiences and better lives if it were an integral part of their schools; however, this belief is essential as an organizing force for everything we do in schools for disadvantaged children.

Students will begin to believe in their own effort-based ability as well. They will work harder and smarter because they come to believe it is worth their while to do so, and they have been taught explicitly *how* to do so. They put care, quality, and craftsmanship above speed (Saphier & D'Auria, 1993). Students do not interpret errors and difficulty as confirmations of their ineptitude (Dweck, 2000.) They look for ways to get help and strategies to overcome obstacles. They have, in short, become believers in their own capacity to grow their abilities and do well if they put forth effective effort.

The transformations I have described seem awesome. There is a tendency to think that only heroes and heroic measures can accomplish this for disadvantaged children. My argument is that expertise and commitment—not heroism—can bring aspiration and achievement to our underserved youth. The purpose of this chapter is to profile this expertise and provide strategies for building the belief system in which it is grounded. I will start with a discussion of the skills and practices of a school focused on effort-based ability.

Part One: Putting Effort-Based Ability to Work

In schools that embody effort-based ability, *all* students receive the three crucial messages mentioned previously, and they receive them at every turn from every adult and from the policies, practices, and procedures of the institution. These crucial messages say:

1. What we're doing here is important.

2. You can do it!

3. I'm not going to give up on you—even if you give up on yourself.

Students come to know that effective effort is the main determinant of achievement—not innate ability.

The "You can do it!" message is not easily accepted by students who are behind academically. A generation of research (Dweck, 2000; Weiner, 1974) on attribution theory tells us that most low-performing students have already concluded that their difficulty in reading, writing, and mathematics is attributable to their low ability. When they succeed at a task, they tend to attribute their success to luck or easy work. We have to teach these students explicitly how to exert effective effort and structure their work so they can see progress, and we must do "attribution retraining" to get them to attribute their performance primarily to their effort.

There are particular arenas of school life—a site, setting, place, or event—that occur frequently where we can see these messages being sent and attribution retraining taking place. The messages are sent through language and choice of words— through the observable things people say and do. They appear in the following seven arenas of interactive teaching behaviors:

- Patterns of calling on students

- Responses to student answers

- Giving help

- Dealing with errors

- Giving tasks and assignments

- Offering feedback on student performance

- Displaying tenacity

Interactive Teaching Behaviors

Patterns of calling on students. Teachers call equally on all students and do not "dumb down" questions or the demand for thinking. Students are treated equally with regard to smiles, nods, eye contact, wait time, and encouragement (Cooper, 1979).

Responses to student answers. Questions are important: they regulate the level of thinking. How we respond after a student has answered, however, may be even more important than the question itself. These responses to student answers set a tone in the room about whether it is safe to take risks, answer if one is not sure, or take on a question that is difficult. Students also reach conclusions about whether or not teachers believe they are able and worthwhile by how we structure our responses. Teachers who act from a belief in effort-based ability keep their focus on the individual student who is asked a question, even if the student responds incorrectly or is silent. Such teachers manifest a pattern of sticking with students who respond incorrectly by using such behaviors as:

- Cueing

- Wait-time

- Expressing confidence

- Asking the question in a different way

- Validating what is right about a student's answer while pointing in another direction

- Asking a student to explain his or her thinking in coming up with the answer

Teachers need not *always*, in *every* situation, stick with a student who responds incorrectly. "Moving on" is not necessarily a sign of "bad" teaching. But sticking with students is, in fact, a dominant *pattern* of teachers who are confidence builders and encourage risk-taking. It is their norm to stick with students who do not answer immediately with the correct response.[1]

Giving help.[2] Teachers are alert for students who are having difficulty, but they are wary of offering unsolicited help, which can be interpreted by students as a lack of confidence in their ability. Teachers choose their language carefully so as to attribute capacity to students and give useful cues:

- Teacher: "What part don't you understand?"

- Student: "I just don't get it."

- Teacher: "Well, the first part is just like the last problem you did. Then we add one more variable. See if you can find out what it is and I'll come back in a few minutes."

Dealing with errors. Teachers cue and correct student errors in such a way as to preserve student dignity and attribute capacity: "That's not quite right, but I'm glad you said that because others thought the same thing. Take a look at these two angles, Ashley. I think you can figure out what they are."

---

[1]For additional examples of sticking with students, see *The Skillful Teacher* by J. Saphier and G. Gower (1997).

[2]For detailed analyses and examples of these arenas, see the "Expectations" chapter of *The Skillful Teacher* by J. Saphier and G. Gower (1997).

Giving tasks and assignments. The language teachers choose acknowledges difficulty where appropriate and highlights areas for focus: "Several of these will be more difficult than usual, but you'll do well if you focus on identifying relevant from irrelevant information."

Offering feedback on student performance. The feedback teachers give to students is nonjudgmental and useful for correcting or improving their work. Peer feedback and self-evaluation are part of the mechanics of classroom design. Answer books, computer resources, tutors, and other adults are available to ensure that feedback is frequent. Cumulative records of student scores and other records of progress are updated continually. These records are always available to students so they know exactly where they stand.

Displaying tenacity. Teachers employ multiple devices to follow up with students who are confused, late with work, unmotivated, unproductive, or otherwise need encouragement. This tenacity can be seen in the number of appointments held with a student, comments of encouragement made in the hall, and in notes and phone calls to the student's home. For example, when Mr. Martinez waves at José as the bus departs from the curb, he says, "And you have your biology book with you, right?"

Classroom Structures and Procedures

Classroom structures and procedures also are vehicles for attribution retraining and for sending the three messages. These include grading, re-teaching loops, redos and retakes, grouping, and rewards.

Grading. Suppose the only grades given are A, B, and "Not Yet." A means the student has gone above and beyond what is called for. B means the student is proficient: a three on a four-point scale. "Not Yet" means that the student's work is not yet at standard. For an end-of-course grade, "Not Yet" means that the course is not finished. The implication of this grading scheme is that proficiency is the only acceptable goal. Modifications of this scheme can be made—perhaps an A, B, C, and "Not Yet" system. Nevertheless, the spirit and the implementation of the grading system are important for conveying to students that the school and teachers believe that the standard matters and that students are capable of attaining it. Such a grading system must be paired with re-teaching loops.

Re-teaching loops. Teachers who use this strategy are talented at identifying individuals or small groups of students who have not mastered skills or information. They use this strategy on a daily basis and create events in which students are re-taught the material in another way. The re-teaching may take place in short small-group instruction the next day while the class is working on other useful assignments; it may take place during free periods, lunch, or after-school tutorials. It is *always* framed without blame or the implication of low ability. Teachers who are most developed at doing re-teaching loops give recognition and status to students who self-nominate because they have self-evaluated and taken the initiative to help close their own learning gaps.

Redos and retakes. Students are encouraged to redo papers and retake tests to raise their grades. When they do, they receive the highest grade they have attained, not an average of all their attempts. As Linda Hunt of Bonnie Eagle High School in Standish, Maine, often says, "There are enough A's for everyone!" Teachers often put constraints on retake procedures, such as: "You have to come to an extra help session before you're allowed to retake the test." Retakes also require that teachers create alternate forms of each major test—a burden that can be lessened by having teams of teachers work together to develop multiple forms of tests.

Grouping. Groupings are made to address students' particular skill needs. They are not permanent and are not based on assessment of overall ability. Who is in what group changes depending on mastery of the skill being taught. Procedures and teacher language convey to students that groupings are all about student mastery—not a label of their ability.

Rewards. Student academic progress is rewarded, and rewards are both desirable and authentically available to all students, regardless of their performance level. For example, at the end of each week in a fourth-grade classroom, a small ritual recognizes students who have reached proficiency with a skill(s) and a note is sent home to their parents identifying the skill. In a middle school, the principal sends a personal letter home once a week to parents of a few children who have exerted effective effort and shown progress. The teachers in each team who nominate students for these letters include data on student progress so the principal can be specific in his or her letter. A high school with a very active math lab appoints students to be tutors for specific skills with which others are having trouble. The students chosen to be tutors include low-performing students who have authentically mastered a skill; they become tutors for that particular skill. Teachers go out of their way to find such students, and the students like being found because being a math tutor five times will get their name on a plaque in the trophy case.

Classroom Climate and Personal Relationship Building

Teachers who are committed to effort-based ability extend themselves to build personal relationships with students.[3]

In addition, teachers work explicitly with a plan to build a classroom climate characterized by:

- Community

- Ownership

- Risk-taking

I have written at length about the strategies and skills teachers can use when they wish to build a classroom climate with these three features (Saphier & Gower, 1997). It is very useful to think about the developmental growth of all three features—from simple to complex over the course of a school year. The figure on page 97 summarizes the developmental stages that thoughtful teachers can work through. Gene Stanford, a high school teacher, first wrote at length about the developmental approach to class climate (Stanford, 1977). A number of excellent programs provide staff development aimed at systematically building class climate. The Northeast Foundation for Children in Greenfield, Massachusetts, and The Stone Center at Wellesley College in Wellesley, Massachusetts, are two such programs.

The small schools movement for secondary schools is largely motivated by a desire to create conditions where these four aspects of classroom climate can be a real part of students' experience. School structures can be explicitly designed to

---

[3]For detailed examples, see the "Personal Relationship Building" chapter of *The Skillful Teacher* by J. Saphier and G. Gower (1997). Also see the "Caring Relationships: The Main Thing" chapter of *Beating the Odds* by J. Ancess (2003).

Creating a Climate of High Achievement for All Students

Community and Mutual Support	Confidence and Risk Taking	Influence and Control
• Knowing others	Mistakes are a sign of weakness. ⬆ Mistakes help one learn.	• Students are empowered to influence the pace of the class.
• Greeting, acknowledging, listening, responding, and affirming	Speed counts. Faster = Smarter ⬆ Care, perseverance, and craftsmanship count.	• Students negotiate the rules of the "classroom game."
• Group identity, responsibility, and interdependence	Good students do it by themselves. ⬆ Good students need help and a lot of feedback.	• Students are taught to use the principles of learning and other learning strategies.
• Cooperative learning, social skills, class meetings, group dynamics	Inborn intelligence is the main determinant of success. ⬆ Effort and effective strategies are the main determinants of success.	• Students use knowledge of learning styles and make choices.
• Problem solving and conflict resolution	Only the bright few can achieve at a high level. ⬆ Everyone is capable of high achievement.	• Students and their communities are sources of knowledge.

(Saphier & D'Auria, 1993)

make community more possible for students. Even in small schools, each individual teacher needs to attend to the climate of his or her own class and gather the skills and strategies needed to do so. This is an excellent task for collaborative teams of teachers.

Explicit Teaching of Effective Effort to All Students

Effective effort has the six attributes of time, focus, resourcefulness, strategies, use of feedback, and commitment[4]:

- **Time.** Students must put in enough minutes and hours to get the job done and understand how much time is required for quality work.

- **Focus.** Work time should be efficient and lacking in distraction. Students may need their teacher's help in creating these conditions at home. Guided imagery exercises to help them maneuver through a chaotic household can be helpful.

- **Resourcefulness.** Students are willing to reach out for help and know how to do so.

- **Strategies.** Students know and use appropriate strategies to handle academic tasks.

- **Use of Feedback.** Good students listen to and look carefully at the feedback they receive from teachers and use it to improve their performance.

- **Commitment.** Effective effort is grounded in will. Students must want to accomplish something to put forth the effort and organize themselves to complete a tough

---

[4]This list was first developed by Jeff Howard of the Efficacy Institute in Waltham, Massachusetts.

learning task. They do not have to like it, but they must be committed to trying hard.

We need to think about these six items as topics in a curriculum. This means we explicitly and directly teach students how to manage time, how to focus themselves, how and where to go when they are stuck, and how to use feedback. These items are woven through the regular curriculum.

What role can we play as teachers in helping students understand the importance of commitment and in helping them to mobilize themselves to succeed? Goal setting is a big part of this role. Teaching students how to set goals that are specific, challenging, attainable, written, and revisited helps support their commitment (see Schunk and Gaa, 1981, and Saphier and Gower, 1997). When teachers ask students to set goals and review them frequently, students obtain the techniques they need to track their progress. This also encourages students to self-evaluate and brings them in contact with their teachers frequently to share their evaluation and data.

We can also help generate student confidence and commitment by incorporating attribution statements about effort and ability into our feedback to students. "You showed you have the brain power to do hard word problems last week. There must be some strategy you aren't using yet that would be the breakthrough on these. Let's take a look . . ."

Students' capacity to show focus and use feedback depends in large part on their teachers. Students must have a clear idea of what the focus is—the precise instructional objective. Creating clear images of the performance we want from students is important. It means more than simply verbalizing the objective; it means showing students what meeting it would look like.

The literature confirms that students do significantly better in academic work when their teachers explicitly teach them strategies for improving reading comprehension; organizing and revising writing; and reviewing, remembering, and summarizing (Paris, Wasik, & Turner, 1991; Pressley, Borkowski, & Schneider, 1987). Parallel literature is available for teaching strategies in math. Readers may be familiar with the names of some of these strategies, such as reciprocal teaching, SQ3R, and the mnemonic keyword technique.

School-Wide Structures for Building a Student Culture of Aspiration, Effective Effort, and Responsibility

The student culture in school can be shaped by adults around the values of academic focus, aspiration, respect, and responsibility. Any staff, regardless of economic and social conditions of students, can do this. Visit North Star Academy, a grade 5–12 school in inner-city Newark, New Jersey, or a dozen others like it around the country to see the proof. Shaping such a student culture is hard work and requires knowledge and skill. The difficulty is often directly proportional to the size of the school—the larger the school, the harder the transformation. Although the forms and practices can vary widely, the principles that successful schools follow in doing this work are consistent.

Motivational boot camp. One effective strategy is motivational boot camp. Have all incoming students (fifth or sixth graders in middle school or ninth graders at the high school level) take a motivational boot camp for 2 weeks in the summer. Although you can also use this strategy with students already enrolled in the school, it will still take several years to build a strong base of motivation within the school.

Motivational boot camp introduces a set of themes that are noticeable every day in the school—not just contained in this 2-week experience:

- First, it creates images for students of others who look and sound like them who have risen in life through education. This gives students positive role models and heroes who are leaders and have accomplished admirable goals.

- Second, it introduces students to the concept of setting goals for themselves and making plans of action to accomplish the goals.

- Third, it builds a strong sense of community among students that is characterized by a sense of psychological safety, team spirit, ownership, and responsibility to the group and the community. This is manifested visibly in the routines and rituals of the school, such as carefully crafted all-school meetings held daily.

- Fourth, it implements a tangible reward system and creates rituals and symbols that emphasize the value of effective effort and academic achievement.

- Fifth, it implements a very tight response system for dealing with distracting and disrespectful behavior.

Why would students be motivated to invest in being a part of this culture of aspiration, effective effort, and responsibility? Because . . .

- Someone who cares about them wants them to succeed.

- They believe they are able to do well.

- They know what to work on to do well. They know what good work looks like and where their current performance is in relation to it.

- They know how to exert effort; they have the strategies and resourcefulness to do so.

- The student peer culture permits them to be seen working hard at academics without social penalty. At best, the student culture supports and encourages academic effort.

- They believe it would be worthwhile to do well.

In schools populated by Masters of Motivation, each of the following school-wide structures might also be addressed directly:

- **Assignment of teachers.** The most skilled teachers are assigned to the students who are the furthest behind.

- **Course schedules.** Adjustments to semester schedules are made to enable students at the "Not Yet" level to attain proficiency. For example, a 2-week "Not Yet" period could be the final 2 weeks of each course in a high school. Students who are already at proficiency in the essential skills and concepts would receive extension and enrichment work during that time. Those who are not would receive additional instruction.

- **Grouping.** The lowest-level tracks are eliminated. Advanced placement courses are open to any student who wants to enroll. Many courses formerly reserved only for college prep and high-performing students are open to mixed groups (Mathews, 1999).

- **Identification of at-risk students and the provision of extra help.** A "pyramid" of identification and intervention structures that go far beyond the typical advisory programs can have a dramatic effect on student achievement. These structures include summer skills programs for incoming students; examination of records every 3 weeks by teaching teams to identify students who are failing or falling behind; personal pairing of faculty members with at-risk students for mentoring; mentoring programs between older and younger students; mandatory tutoring for identified students; and guided study periods based on contracts between students, teachers, and parents. For details and examples at all grade levels, I refer readers to the superb compendium of strategies in *Whatever It Takes* (DuFour, DuFour, Eaker, and Karhanek, 2004).

A Focus on the Future

Students may not believe that what they are learning in school has much bearing on what they will do in their future lives. Middle-class children tend to work at least hard enough to pass since they see a college degree as a ticket to a decent life and a well-paying career. But a large number of working class and poor children do not aspire to this. Not everyone has to go to college (though all who want to should have the chance), but everyone needs to graduate from high school with adequate skills for functioning in the 21st Century workplace and the credentials they need to pursue post-secondary education. The "Jobs for the Future" program (www.jff.org/jff) does a good job of giving students these images while they are still in high school and the images can have a positive impact on their graduation rate. Much more could be done in high schools, such as the work done by the American Diploma Project (www.achieve.org/achieve.nsf/AmericanDiplomaProject), to give students insight into their futures and motivate them to take their studies more seriously.

Parent involvement is also a critical component to effort-based ability. In disadvantaged communities, schools need to approach the parents instead of expecting them to come to the school. Have families host small gatherings of parents in their apartments where school personnel can share the school's academic expectations, talk about the importance of homework, and most importantly, give parents a vision of what a good education can do for their children. Overwhelmed parents may not be able to help with homework or help their children devote time to it. Too many of our children have to assume adult-like childcare responsibilities for younger siblings and respond to other family needs. But if parents value doing well in school, that message will be communicated often enough to their children to make a difference.

Part Two: Building and Strengthening the Belief in Effort-Based Ability

What do school leaders do if their staff members do not believe that "smart is something you can get"? What if the majority of teachers believe in the bell curve of intelligence and recreate it through their actions?

Michael Fullan believes that we can act our way to new beliefs. This is true, but school leaders often encounter stiff opposition to acting in new ways if these new ways challenge long-held beliefs. So how do we change people's beliefs?

Well, we do not change them—at least not literally. People have to change their own beliefs. But we can have a significant effect on them. Here is how: take a belief that you think is critical to your school's success and . . .

- Say it
- Model it
- Organize for it
- Protect it
- Reward it[5]

Say It

At every possible opportunity, express what *you* believe about effort-based ability and what you think it can do for the children in your school. Sometimes these are public occasions; other times they are small group or private conversations. These constant expressions about the importance of a belief are very powerful forces for others who are considering that belief and beginning to align their behavior with it. Leaders often underestimate the power of simply standing for something publicly and with perseverance.

- Develop a short speech and some concise statements you believe in so you can speak convincingly about the issue.

- Use words that do not stifle opposition or the expression of disbelief—you must keep the door open to dialog.

- Include a motivational quote or paragraph in every parent newsletter and class newsletter.

---

[5] I have found this framework valuable for three decades as a leader in building norms and beliefs in my own organizations. I would love to credit Edgar Shein with this formulation, because for decades I thought it was his. He denies it, however. The original author is unknown to me.

- Talk about the significance of effort-based ability in your public remarks to staff.

- Talk about the significance of effort-based ability at back-to-school night in your welcome speech to parents.

- Use posters that list the attributes of effective effort in the halls or in other appropriate and visible places throughout the school.

- Get your leadership team on board by putting this topic on the agenda of every meeting, even if only to check in on progress: "What have you seen?" "What have you or your team members done?"

Model It

Build visible action from this belief into your own practice. The following strategies and other similar actions show that you really mean it:

- Teach a class in effective effort to a group of students.

- Give teachers feedback on how they send the three crucial messages and use the arenas for attribution retraining. Build the sending of these messages into teacher evaluation criteria.

- Model your own openness to taking risks and making and correcting errors by sharing when this happens with staff.

- Be seen and heard in one classroom every day talking to a student about something he or she is working on and making positive attribution statements about that work.

- Let others see and hear you learning something new.

Organize for It

Create structures or events that spring from a belief in effort-based ability.

- Hold a staff development day for all staff or for team leaders on the history of intelligence, the bell curve, and effort-based ability with convincing data about the malleability of intelligence.

- Make it a priority to examine the test/retest/retake policy and practices in your school for grading in grade-level or subject teams.

- Identify incoming students who are at risk. Choose teachers for them who are the most committed to effort-based ability; provide extra funds in the budget for them.

- Institute a required after-school homework study hall for those students who did not do their homework. During this study hall, students do the homework assigned on that day.

- Form a committee to develop a curriculum for teaching students about effective effort. See the Efficacy Institute's curriculum *Your "Get Smart" Toolkit* (www.efficacy.org).

- Do staff development on classroom interactions for accomplishing attribution retraining.

- Create ways to acknowledge or reward students who persevere and correct the errors in their homework or classwork.

- Structure a faculty meeting where teachers read and discuss case studies on educators who changed children's lives through deliberate attribution retraining. Start a follow-up study group where people share their ongoing experiences with attribution retraining and getting students to change their views of themselves.

- Train parent volunteers and aides in how to respond to student answers and errors and provide motivating help.

- Build "Not Yet" periods into schedules where students receive intensive tutoring in concepts not yet mastered. Reward students who decide to attend these sessions on their own, without being sent by a teacher.

- Provide site visits for students to mentors in the community who can testify to the role of education in their success. Show how literacy and math skills are used in the workplace.

Protect It

Stand behind teachers who implement practices that may generate negative feedback from peers, such as giving students the highest grades they achieve without averaging the scores of their retakes.

- At budget time, put a "fence" around resources allocated to support effort-based ability structures.

- Build community support for these structures and practices by presenting information on them to the school board and community clubs and agencies.

- Invite the press to feature stories on your school's effort-based practices and structures.

Reward It

Provide students and teachers with appropriate recognition for acting on their belief in effort-based ability.

- Reward younger students nominated by their teachers for demonstrating effective effort. "Pizza With the Principal" is one possible reward.

- Reward older students for academic improvement with off-campus privileges or another special privilege.

- Recognize teachers who build effort-based ability into their practice with personal notes, commendations for their files, and, when appropriate, public recognition to the school board or in newsletters.

- Support these teachers who build effort-based ability into their practice in ways consistent with the belief by inviting them to attend conferences or other staff development opportunities.

The following exercise is a useful way to introduce the idea of effort-based ability to a staff. Ask staff members to think of an area where they "know" they are not able. (All of us have some area where we believe we have no gifts—"I can't sing . . . do math . . . mix at parties . . . speak in public, etc.") Then ask people to remember the time when they first became convinced they had no talent in that area. Have them take notes on the following:

1. What was the event?

2. What happened and who said what?

3. What feelings did you have?

4. What were the consequences?

After giving people 3 or 4 minutes to take notes silently on their memories, ask them to share in small groups.

It is remarkable how vivid these memories often are—how powerful the stories are although they may have happened decades ago. Often the consequence people report is that they never tried again. This exercise illustrates the degree to which we all accept external messages about our ability and avoid areas where we feel that we are defective based on scant but searing evidence. If the area of functioning happens to be reading or academic ability, the consequences for a young person can be devastating and life-altering.

This exercise can be used to initiate a series of faculty forums, shared readings,[6] study groups, and informal conversations that are constantly fed by the reading of articles and books and participation in workshops that leaders organize over a period of time. In doing so, leaders will find that their own conviction and clarity to apply the "Say It, Model It, Organize for It, Protect It, and Reward It" model will be strengthened.

Building Engines of Hope

Many students in poor communities are up to four grade levels behind (Thernstrom & Thernstrom, 2003.) They may live in neighborhoods where low aspirations and bad role models for survival in adult life are the norm. But whatever the disadvantages and the obstacles, students are not held back by inherent intellectual deficiency. If the adults in these schools

---

[6]Suggestions: David Perkins' *Outsmarting IQ*; Jeff Howard's *The Social Construction of Intelligence*; Stephen Jay Gould's *The Mismeasure of Man*; Lauren Resnick's "From Aptitude to Effort: A New Foundation for Our Schools" (1995), *Daedalus*, *124*(4), 55–62.

can act with vigor and perseverance and apply the best practices developed in recent decades, they can make life-changing differences for their students—despite their disadvantages.

It is well documented that in the worst circumstances imaginable, individual schools can rebuild themselves as engines of ability creation and academic achievement for the most disadvantaged students (Charles Dana Center, 1999; Jerald, 2001; Minkoff, 2003; NASSP, 2004). The life cycle of these schools tends to be short—a decade typically from rise to fall. This is a shame, and it is unnecessary. The same cycles of up and down characterize many of our schools in less dramatic ways and in less disadvantaged communities. In every case I know, what rose and fell was not the curriculum, the safety of the neighborhood, or the resources at the school's disposal. It was the leadership among the adults in the school.

Strong professional learning communities produce schools that are engines of hope and achievement for students. They do not come into being by accident. There is nothing more important for education in the decades ahead than educating and supporting leaders in the commitments, understanding, and skills necessary to grow such schools where a focus on effort-based ability is the norm. This means paying serious attention to the preparation, licensure, evaluation, and continual professional development of school leaders. Our best schools cannot create sustainable change if the clarity and skills of their leaders about how to build PLCs are transient, unmonitored, and underdeveloped. But we now understand these skills, and it is time we put that understanding to work.

References

Ancess, J. (2003). *Beating the odds.* New York: Teachers College Press.

Charles A. Dana Center. (1999). *Hope for urban education: A study of nine high-performing, high-poverty, urban elementary schools.* Austin, TX: Author.

Cooper, H. M. (1979). Pygmalion grows up: A model of teacher expectations, communication, and performance influence. *Review of Educational Research, 49,* 389–410.

DuFour, R., DuFour, R., Eaker, R., & Karhanek, G. (2004). *Whatever it takes: How professional learning communities respond when kids don't learn.* Bloomington, IN: Solution Tree (formerly National Educational Service).

Dweck, C. S. (2000). *Self-theories: Their role in motivation, personality and development.* Philadelphia: Psychology Press.

Jerald, C. D. (2001). *Dispelling the myth revisited: Preliminary findings from a nationwide analysis of "high-flying" schools.* Washington, DC: The Education Trust.

Mathews, J. (1999, March 6). Teacher closes the achievement gap: In Alexandria school, classes in government mix students of all levels. *Washington Post,* p. B1.

Minkoff, M. (2003). *Head of the class: Characteristics of higher performing urban high schools in Massachusetts.* Boston: Center for Education Research and Policy at Mass INC.

National Association of Secondary School Principals (NASSP). (2004). *Breakthrough high schools: You can do it, too!* (Vol. 1). Reston, VA: Author.

Newmann, F., & Wehlage, G. (1995). *Successful school restructuring.* Madison, WI: Center on Organization and Restructuring of Schools.

Paris, S., Wasik, B., & Turner, J. (1991). The development of strategic readers. In R. Barr, M. Kamil, P. Modenthal, & P. D. Pearson (Eds.), *Handbook of reading research* (Vol. 2, pp. 609–640). New York: Longman.

Pressley, M., Borkowski, J., & Schneider, W. (1987). Cognitive strategies: Good strategy users coordinate metacognition and knowlege. In R. Vasta & G. Whitehurst (Eds.), *Annals of Child Development, 5,* 89–129.

Saphier, J. (2005). *John Adams' promise*. Acton, MA: Research for Better Teaching.

Saphier, J., & D'Auria, J. (1993). *How to bring vision to school improvement*. Acton, MA: Research for Better Teaching.

Saphier, J., D'Auria, J., & King, M. (2004). *Teams are windows into the soul of a school*. Manuscript submitted for publication.

Saphier, J., & Gower, R. R. (1997). *The skillful teacher*. Acton, MA: Research for Better Teaching.

Saphier, J. D., & King, M. (1985). Good seeds grow in strong cultures. *Educational Leadership, 42*(6), 67–74.

Schunk, D. H., & Gaa, J. P. (1981). Goal-setting influence on learning and self-evaluation. *Journal of Classroom Interaction, 16*, 38–44.

Stanford, G. (1977). *Developing effective classroom groups*. New York: Hart Publishing.

Thernstrom, A., & Thernstrom, S. (2003). *No excuses: Closing the racial gap in learning*. New York: Simon and Schuster.

Weiner, B. (1974). *Achievement motivation and attribution theory*. Morristown, NJ: General Learning Press.

Roland S. Barth

No contemporary educational author has offered more thoughtful and insightful observations on the role of the principal in shaping a productive school culture than Dr. Roland Barth. As the founder and former director of Harvard University Principals' Center and the International Network of Principals' Centers, he has helped bring attention to the complexity of the principalship and the need for principals to continue their learning in a collaborative environment. He has shared his expertise in the highly acclaimed books *Lessons Learned, Learning by Heart, Improving Schools from Within,* and *Run School Run.* A recurring theme of his work has been a consistent challenge to educators to improve their schools from within by redefining their roles, responsibilities, and relationships.

In this chapter, Dr. Barth calls attention to how schools have traditionally addressed the question, "How will we respond when students don't learn?" He contends that educators have developed an arsenal of punitive measures when students do not learn and have consistently conveyed the message "learn or we will punish you." He expresses concern that this use of punishment for not learning is becoming more commonplace and severe with the increased emphasis on high-stakes tests. He regards this use of coercion as inconsistent with the mission of schooling to create lifelong learners. He laments the preoccupation with grades and test performance and warns that a consequence is students who are turned off to learning.

Dr. Barth is convinced that the most fundamental best practice of a professional learning community is the promotion of insatiable, lifelong learning in every member of the school community. He provides specific examples of what such a culture would look like and offers suggestions to educators for monitoring their students' growth as lifelong learners.

Dr. Roland Barth is a consultant to schools, school districts, state departments of education, universities, foundations, and businesses in the United States and abroad. He can be reached at rsb44@aol.com.

Chapter 6

Turning Book Burners Into Lifelong Learners

Roland S. Barth

First I saw the smoke, then the fire. In the alley stood a half dozen high school students pitching books, notes, and papers into a flaming trash can. I approached the group with the worry of a former principal to find out what was going on.

"We're burning our notes and books," they said. "We're outta there!" Final exams were over and nothing but graduation lay ahead for these seniors. They were celebrating. Upon further inquiry, I learned that these were A and B students, most headed to college in a few months.

This encounter deeply troubled me—and it still does today. What did it mean? What does it say about 13 years of heroic efforts to educate students by scores of teachers, counselors, administrators, and parents? It brought to mind a common definition of an "at-risk" student: a student who leaves school with little likelihood of continuing learning. To me, these honor students were at risk.

Learning and Punishment

In pondering this incendiary moment, it now occurs to me that beneath the culture of all too many schools, school systems, and even universities lurks a very chilling message to students: "Learn or we will punish you." Educators have succeeded handsomely in coupling human learning—a natural energy with which all of us enter the world and school—with an astonishing arsenal of punitive measures:

> "Eddie, if you don't get your multiplication tables memorized, you will repeat fourth grade."

> "Kiesha, if you don't raise your score on the standardized test, you won't graduate."

> "Marcus, if you don't get to work on your social studies project, I'm calling your parents."

> "If you don't pass the state test, you will go to summer school."

And so it goes: "Learn or we will punish you." As I reflect further on that roaring fire, I suspect that those students were really telling us this: "You can't hurt me anymore." They were exhilarated to be rid of the threats hanging over their heads. By tightly coupling learning and punishment in our schools, we cause students to dismiss the good along with the bad.

Under the specter of high-stakes tests and No Child Left Behind, teachers and administrators continue to ratchet up the punishments for *not* learning. To their credit, students are spending more time preparing for and taking tests, and they are jumping over higher and higher bars. Considerable evidence attests that achievement scores across the country *are*

rising—to the satisfaction of many policy makers, board members, parents, and educators.

But there are tragic and enduring costs. If a school succeeds in getting 80% of its students to score at the 80th percentile, and if the consequence is more students who burn their books literally (as a few do, as I have witnessed) and figuratively (as we know many do), then we are winning some battles but losing the more important war. If a school culture permeated by preoccupation with grades and test performance forever turns students off to learning, then the cost of short-term success is long-term failure. As one researcher who looked at the effects of giving students low grades found, "Instead of prompting greater effort, zeros and the low grades they yield more often cause students to withdraw from learning" (Guskey, 2004).

I once saw an estimate that 50 years ago students graduated from high school knowing 75% of what they would need to know for the rest of their lives—in the workplace, in their families, and for life in general. The estimate today is that graduates of our schools leave knowing perhaps 2% of what they will need to know in the future. And yet they leave school today knowing far more than they did 50 years ago. As we have learned, knowledge doubles every 3 years; technology goes through a new generation every 18 months. The concept that one can learn, once and for all, all the information and skills needed for life, if it ever had merit, clearly no longer does. John Dewey stated it perfectly nearly a century ago: "The most important attitude that can be formed is that of the desire to go on learning" (Littky, 2004, p. 38).

Clearly the most basic graduation requirement, then, is that our students leave each grade and each school imbued with the qualities, dispositions, and capacities of insatiable, lifelong learners. The students who do will acquire that 98% yet to come and will thrive. Those who burn their books will be relegated to the periphery of the 21st Century.

Lifelong Learning

I would like to suggest that a most fundamental best practice in a professional learning community is to promote the qualities and dispositions of insatiable, lifelong learning in every member of the school community—young people and adults alike—so that when the school experience concludes, learning will not.

"Lifelong learning" means many things to many people. When I say lifelong learning, I mean:

- A love of learning for its own sake

- A voluntary engagement in learning activities

- The ability to ask one's own questions and take responsibility for addressing and pursuing them

- The ability to marshal resources to address those questions: time, attention, money, tools, other people, books, technology

- The ability to sustain engagement over time

- The capacity to continuously reflect on oneself as a learner and on the learning

- The capacity to set one's own high standards of learning and to assess the extent to which one is succeeding in resolving the question posed

- The capacity to know and celebrate success

In short, as George Bernard Shaw once said, "What we want to see is the child in pursuit of knowledge, and not knowledge in pursuit of the child" (Littky, 2004, p. 5).

Let me offer some examples of lifelong learning. With his colleagues, Dennis Littky (2004) founded The Met, a collection of small secondary schools in Providence, Rhode Island. He offers a glimpse of what lifelong learning might look like in a school:

- A ninth grader who "hates science" sees a movie about freezing people and then decides to read a college biology text on cryogenics. He then gives a very impressive presentation on the subject to the class.

- A student who has never been serious about anything to do with school starts staying after every day because she is so wrapped up in a project that *she chose to do* on nonviolence and the civil rights movement that she just cannot put it down.

This is what lifelong learning might look like within a school context—students who feel compelled to learn on their own because of their interest and excitement. Examples of this lifelong learning abound in the world outside of school. We simply have to look around to notice them.

Consider the following:

- A retired college professor decides to take voice lessons and participates in a small recital with his fellow students.

- Millions of adults participate in television celebrity Oprah Winfrey's vastly influential national book club.

- A woman takes a week of sailing lessons designed exclusively for women so that she can feel more confident sailing with a mixed crew.

In all of these cases, the individuals pose their own questions, marshal resources, and work with passion and direction to address them. How badly we need more similar examples in our schools.

The Principal and Lifelong Learning

What would happen if a school took seriously the goal of promoting profound levels of learning and graduating students destined to sustain prodigious levels of learning over their lifetimes? How might one create within a school culture a community of lifelong learners? As in most whole school reform efforts, the school principal must lead the way. But what does that mean?

Model lifelong learning. As Gandhi said, "We must be the change we wish to see in the world." School leaders must persistently exhibit, model, and celebrate lifelong learning themselves. Students are not dumb; they look at the most important role models in their lives and say, "I want to be like that!" If they see adults who are all finished learning, they too will want to be finished learning. If they see adults who are constantly asking questions, reading, sharing good ideas, and posing and solving problems, so will they.

In my visits to schools, I have observed principals engaging in simple yet transformative activities that support a culture of lifelong learning. For example, I met a principal in Broward County, Florida, who demonstrates the incredible power of modeling. She places a sign on her doorknob when she goes off to a meeting or a professional development activity that reads "Out Learning." When she is in her office, she flips the sign over so all passing by can see that she is "In Learning." Either way, she conveys an extraordinary message each day to every student, teacher, and parent who walks by. A host of diplomas, degrees, and certificates on a wall signifies one who is "learned," but this educator's little sign on her door identifies a leading learner in the school—a lifelong learner.

I am now ashamed to admit that as a principal I frequently initiated staff development sessions for the faculty after school, and then, unobtrusively, I tiptoed out of the back of the room and returned to my office to attend to "more important things." Thinking back on it, I see what a toxic, obtrusive message I was sending: "Learning is for unimportant people; important people don't need to learn." The principal who *joins with* the faculty and students in learning activities is the one who changes the school culture into one that is hospitable to lifelong learning.

Build a staff of lifelong learners. A second imperative for the principal who would build a community of lifelong learners is to stock the faculty with lifelong learners. I knew one principal who required evidence of continuing learning as the major criteria for hiring new teachers. I wish I knew more principals like him.

Unfortunately, almost every faculty includes people who show indisputable signs of being "burned out" or "brain dead" and all finished learning. They refuse to attend professional development workshops; they hoard their successes and refuse to exchange best teaching practices with colleagues. The principal must hold high expectations for the learning of every educator in the school—especially these teachers who appear to be all finished learning. The principal who accepts and tolerates a non-learning attitude in a teacher maintains low expectations for this teacher every bit as much as the teacher who holds low expectations for the learning of students from "the wrong side of the tracks" or those deemed not able to succeed for some reason or another. In both cases, low expectations demean, damage, and corrode the learner and his or her ability to learn.

If we truly believe that all children can learn, then we must believe that all educators can learn, even in the face of contrary evidence. I am indebted to two well-worn teachers in a school where I was principal for teaching me this lesson. I had written them off as learners. In their classooms in a remote corner of the third floor, they appeared to keep both their doors and their minds closed. Largely through the efforts of some wonderful colleagues, these two teachers, after many years in hibernation, returned to life as learners.

Their generously spirited fellow teachers successfully encouraged the isolated pair to join them on teaching teams. We then aligned each teacher with an energetic student teacher. We held periodic conversations about the conditions under which each of us learned best. Then we attempted to provide these conditions for ourselves and for one another. All of us—not only the formerly "at-risk" teachers—came to imbed the qualities of the lifelong learner in our daily work.

This experience taught me to replace the question, "Can this teacher learn?" with another more hopeful and demanding question: "Under what conditions that I can devise will this person come back to life as a learner?" If we are inventive and persistent and hold *high* expectations, I believe we can always find those conditions. There is no higher calling for the school leader than to ensure that every member of the staff is a voracious learner. This brings a precious gift to the students, the school, and to the teachers themselves: membership in good standing of a professional learning community.

Place lifelong learning in sight. It is one thing for the adults within the school to be learners; it is quite another for them to make their learning visible. Unfortunately, most of the time educators spend learning is out of sight of others. For instance, a teacher takes a course on weekends, attends a professional development conference, or reads the professional literature at home. Teachers such as this may indeed be lifelong learners, but only when they disclose their learning will they fully foster lifelong learning in others.

We are all familiar with the teacher who asks students to write an essay on "what I learned over the summer." One principal in Oregon decided to devote the entire first issue of the school newsletter to teachers' (and her own) learning. At the close of summer, she asked each staff member to write a few lines about "what I learned over the summer."

All of a sudden an entire faculty came out of the closet as learners. Many who may not have learned very much of late suddenly engaged in learning activities. Many reflected on themselves as learners and on what they were learning. Needless to say, when the newsletter appeared, students, their parents, and other teachers devoured it with special interest. This was a most inventive form of staff development and a powerful way for the educators to convey the message that learning is what *important* people do. There is no more telling message for students to hear from adults.

If we are serious about young people becoming lifelong learners, then we first must become visible, lifelong learners ourselves. Wonderful things happen when teachers and administrators transform themselves from "the learned" who transmit their knowledge to "the learners" into leading citizens of a community of learners.

Enlist parental participation. One principal worked with his parent group to help transform the school culture into one of lifelong learning. Parents decided to modify their usual dinner table conversation with their children. Instead of asking, "What did you learn in school today?" they exclaimed, "Let me tell you what I learned at work today!" Parents talked about baking bread in a bakery, driving a bus, working in a biology lab, and so on. Students were fascinated, not only to learn more about their parents' work life, but also to discover that their parents were learners—and still learning! Not surprisingly, parents reported that their children began to take learning and school much more seriously. So parents, like educators, can use their influential place as role models in young peoples' lives to much effect.

These are among the ways I have witnessed principals, teachers, and parents transforming their school cultures. When students constantly witness the important adults in their lives as learners, they too will come to value learning at school and beyond. Only a school hospitable to lifelong learning on the part of adults will be a school where lifelong learning flourishes for students.

Students as Lifelong Learners

A backdrop of adult lifelong learning, evident to students 192 days a year, sets the stage for young people to also become lifelong learners. Such a stage is necessary, but not sufficient. In order for schools to graduate students who will be lifelong learners—not book burners—lifelong learning must become a major part of the curriculum. This means that:

- Members of the school community will come to share lifelong learning as a common goal. Every student will show increasing evidence over time of becoming an independent, self-sustained learner. By graduation, *all* students will demonstrate evidence of becoming life-long learners; and

- Schools will have some systematic means of assessing the progress of each student toward this goal.

These days, schools seem to evaluate everything under the sun that deals with student performance: skills in composition, algebra, geography, science, and literacy. Yet I know of no school faculty that attempts to assess the extent to which they are succeeding in developing voracious, lifelong learners. What would happen if a school took as criteria for assessment the qualities of the lifelong learner listed on page 118?

- Loving learning for its own sake
- Engaging in learning on a voluntary basis
- Asking one's own questions and taking responsibility
- Marshalling resources
- Sustaining engagement in learning
- Continuously reflecting

- Assessing one's learning

- Knowing and celebrating successes

How might a school measure not just whether a student is advancing from one grade to the next, but the extent to which students are graduating as at-risk learners or as lifelong, insatiable learners?

The answer, I believe, is very simple, albeit sobering: examine what students do on their own time. Ultimately, real learning—lifelong learning—like character, is what students do when no one is looking. Let me provide some examples:

One high school senior I know is passionately committed to music, specifically to learning and playing the bass guitar. In addition to constantly practicing in his garage, he started his own band with some friends, and last summer drove 100 miles to a music camp for which he paid the tuition by doing chores on my farm. He plans to major in music in college.

Another student, a rather shy young woman, discovered drama as a way of expressing herself. In addition to winning the lead in the high school play, she now participates in local community theater productions. She chose her college program because it included a semester in Europe to study theater.

Yet another student, one with athletic as well as mechanical interests and talents, earned money to buy increasingly complex bikes, which he tinkers with and maintains so that he can participate in "extreme" biking competitions.

Assessing lifelong learning in schools is a novel idea; there are few stories or precedents that offer specific guidance. Constructing ways of detecting, monitoring, and measuring lifelong learning in students is badly needed. There are, however, some promising ideas:

One school asks students to keep a log documenting how they spend their out-of-school time. Parents keep a parallel log detailing how they observe these same children spending their time. This information is discussed between parent and student, bringing keen attention to the subject. The information is then shared with teachers, guidance counselors, and administrators.

In this school community it became very clear, very quickly, which students were participating in learning activities outside of school and which were not. Students were then classified as displaying "no," "little," "some," or "a great deal of" engagement in learning activities on their own time.

The results were both surprising and discouraging. They were surprising because engagement in purposeful learning activities outside of school did not neatly correlate with grade point achievement in school. Some A students in school turned off of learning outside of school; some underachieving students in school came alive as learners outside of school—such as the biker and garage band performer mentioned previously. These are the students who would probably agree with Mark Twain when he said, "I never let my schooling interfere with my education." What was discouraging was that there was precious little evidence of serious, sustained, voluntary, out-of-school learning by any students.

The remedy for students who are turned off to learning is usually more of the same: more didactic instruction, more worksheets, more texts and tests, and more hours in school each day, each week, and each year. These remedies may work in the short term to improve performance, but do so at the expense of curtailing lifelong learning. They carry the threatening message, "perform or we will punish you." Learning is not even an option.

Promoting Lifelong Learners

Let us assume that our professional learning community has come to embrace the goal of lifelong learning for all and information is now available to the PLC that reveals how students spend their own time. Then we are, of course, confronted with a tough and crucial question: "What will educators do when they learn that many students perform well under our direction while at school and then 'burn their books' when they are on their own?" Presently, of course, we do nothing.

When continuous, independent learning for students becomes the goal, a school is forced to engage in some difficult and, I believe, ultimately transformative thinking: Educators will have to examine what is going on in school that seems to be turning students off to learning and determine how to turn them back on.

Give learning a good name. I believe all too many schools give learning a bad name by defining it in a narrow way that is unattractive to students. Ask sixth graders what they think of as "real learning." The usual answer is, "listening to the teacher, reading assignments, working alone filling out worksheets, taking exams, and being graded." Well, if that is all learning is, then I would want to burn my books, too! What about the teacher who is learning to speak a foreign language? Or the fourth grader who is learning to embroider? Or the child who spends every afternoon after school trying to perfect his curve ball? Is that real learning? You bet! Schools give learning a good name when they include, honor, embrace, and make use of all of the many ways that a person comes to know something that he or she cares passionately about.

Pose and answer our own problems. Most of what goes on in schools involves solving someone else's problems. Young people solve algebra problems. They find the causes of the Civil War. They answer the questions the teacher poses for a reading assignment. These are all teachers' problems. There are certainly plenty of circumstances when addressing the teachers' problems is important, even essential, for a student's development. Yet the learning potential in solving someone else's problems is limited. It can foster dependent rather than independent thinking. The problems that we pose for ourselves, care deeply about, are motivated to engage in, and find meaningful are the ones that harbor the greatest opportunities for learning—in the short run while we are in school, and in the long run beyond school. Consequently, I believe learning in schools becomes energized and likely to spread to out-of-school time only when young people have as many opportunities to pose and address their own problems as they do to grapple with problems posed by teachers.

Reduce didactic instruction. The predominant sound heard within the classroom is the voice of the teacher. It has been estimated that 85% of what goes on in schools is teacher-directed, didactic instruction. This enables a transmission of information from the teacher (who presumably has it) to the student (who presumably does not). The other 15% is something else. Unfortunately, ample research suggests that what a person retains a few weeks later is perhaps 5% of what he or she was told. This conventional teaching and learning is a weak strategy, indeed. As the saying goes, "The notes of the lecturer are passed to the notes of the student . . . without going through the minds of either."

If I could do one thing to reform education in North America to help build a community of lifelong learners, it would be to shift the ratio: 15% didactic instruction and 85% something else. Teachers will ask, "But what do I do for 85% of the time if I don't 'instruct' the students?" This is the same question that many teachers facing block schedules with 120 uninterrupted minutes and a group of young people are now asking. It is only when we ask the question, "How can I promote profound levels of human learning other than by talking?" that I believe we really become educators. Nothing will hook students for a lifetime of learning more than what we do with that 85% of their time.

Some schools have indeed reduced the formal teacher instruction way below 85% and introduced a rich repertoire of "something else." Micro Society Schools, a school reform organization based in Philadelphia, Pennsylvania, has created within many schools a community of businesses, banks, courts, and law enforcement systems in which students play real and essential roles. In order to play those roles, students must, of course, learn. It is not a large leap for them to connect the learning done in school to the need for lifelong learning outside of school.

Many schools offer strong programs and activities such as cooperative learning, role playing, drama, ropes courses, field studies, and internships in the community, as well as independent learning activities such as running a school newspaper, coaching a team, tutoring younger children, and assisting the

---

Lifelong Learning Through Expeditionary Learning: The Outward Bound Design Principles

Expeditionary Learning Outward Bound is a proven model for comprehensive school reform for elementary, middle, and high schools. It promotes lifelong learning with its emphasis on learning by doing and its focus on character growth, teamwork, reflection, and literacy.

Teachers connect high-quality academic learning to adventure, service, and character development through a variety of student experiences including interdisciplinary, project-based learning expeditions. Outward Bound's design principles include:

- Self-discovery
- Wonderful ideas
- Responsibility for learning
- Intimacy and caring
- Success and failure
- Collaboration and compassion
- Diversity and inclusivity
- The natural world
- Solitude and reflection
- Service and compassion

For a complete description of these principles, visit Outward Bound's web site at www.elob.org.

---

teacher in creative ways. Sadly, these are increasingly seen as "frills," yet this "something else" is often where the real preparation as a life-long learner takes place.

Promote pleasure and success. I believe schools will succeed in promoting learning and lifelong learners when students find on a regular basis in their school experiences both pleasure and success. This will not happen all the time, of course, because not all learning is pleasant or successful. Much learning comes from unpleasant work and even failure. But students must experience pleasure and success often enough so that they will feel absorbed, committed, and satisfied in their learning. To the extent they find times of pleasure and success in their school learning each day, they will want to experience the same level of pleasure and success in learning activities outside of school. To the extent that they find little pleasure and little success, they will not seek it elsewhere. How to make likely this occurrence of pleasure and success in every student's learning each day is a central challenge to the educator who would promote lifelong learning.

Reward instead of punish. Finally, let me comment again on the link between learning and punishment that is so prevalent in our schools. This leads, as I have suggested, to a culture of "book burners." Schools that take the goal of lifelong learning seriously must find ways to decouple learning from punishment. They must change the underlying message in the school from "Learn or we will punish you" to the better message of "Learn or you will hurt yourself." Even better is: "Learning brings its own rewards." This demands a total rethinking of our systems of rewards and punishments. This means fundamentally changing the teaching experiences of educators and the learning experiences of students in school.

Lifelong Learning as the "Standard"

There is no more difficult and important job for the educator than to change the prevailing culture of a school so that it will become hospitable to learning, both in the classroom and throughout the lives of students, teachers, and parents. Would it not be astonishing if lifelong learning became the "standard" against which schools, school professionals, and students were evaluated? When we develop within our schools such a professional learning community, we will be well on our way toward an even more remarkable accomplishment: building a professional learning community within our society—one where no one burns books!

References

Guskey, T. (2004). 0 alternatives. *Principal Leadership, 5*(2), 49–53.

Littky, D. (2004). *The big picture: Education is everyone's business.* Alexandria, VA: Association for Supervision and Curriculum Development.

Mike Schmoker

Perhaps no one has been more influential in insisting that schools develop a "results orientation" than Dr. Mike Schmoker. His book *Results: The Key to Continuous School Improvement* (1999) became one of the best sellers in the Association for Supervision and Curriculum Development's history. Its companion piece, *The Results Fieldbook: Practical Strategies for Dramatically Improved Schools* (2001), built on his argument that meaningful teamwork, measurable goals, and the regular collection and analysis of student performance data constitute "the foundation for results . . . [that] goad, guide, and motivate groups and individuals" (1999, p. 2).

A former English teacher, football coach, and central office administrator, Dr. Schmoker also served as a senior consultant at the Mid-Continent Regional Educational Laboratory. He has authored three books and numerous articles that have appeared in *Educational Leadership, Phi Delta Kappan, Education Week*, and *TIME Magazine.* He has consulted with school districts throughout the United States and Canada and recently was a featured speaker at the Harvard Principal's Institute.

In this chapter, he asserts that creating PLCs is "the best, least expensive, most professionally rewarding way to improve schools." He regards collaborative teams of teachers as the engine that drives the school improvement process, and he contends that there is overwhelming evidence that schools get better results when teams of professionals plan for, monitor, and celebrate gains in student learning. He calls for a new school culture in which teacher isolation is replaced by the collective autonomy of teaching teams that are willing to accept responsibility for results. He concludes by challenging readers not only to embrace the promise that PLCs offer "immense, unprecedented hope for schools" but to also take the necessary steps to put PLC concepts into action in their own settings.

For more information on Dr. Mike Schmoker and his work, contact him at Schmoker@futureone.com or go to www.mikeschmoker.com.

Chapter 7

No Turning Back: The Ironclad Case for Professional Learning Communities

Mike Schmoker

School success depends, more than anything, on the quality of teaching we provide. Unfortunately, much of the instruction we provide is not what it should be. For one thing, the actual, taught curriculum varies widely from teacher to teacher; many students never even have the opportunity to learn essential knowledge and skills (Berliner, 1984; Marzano, Marzano, & Pickering, 2003). Teachers themselves agree that the actual quality of lessons in many areas is poor or inconsistent; they agree that the most fundamental elements of effective lessons, which most teachers know or have learned, are routinely left out. As a result, one representative study found that "in just one academic year, the top third of teachers produced as much as *six times* the learning growth of the bottom third" (Sparks, 2004, p. 47).

This lack of effectiveness is entirely unnecessary. We have the means to make teaching more effective and consistent than ever before and to create the kinds of schools students deserve. The place to begin is with a set of simple structures and practices that constitute what are now being called "learning communities." As I will attempt to show, this is not a fad. On the contrary, it may represent the richest, most unprecedented culmination of the best we know about authentic school improvement.

What Are "Learning Communities"?

Rick DuFour recently warned that the concept of "learning communities" is at "a critical juncture." The concept is in danger of being misunderstood, and misunderstanding leads to failure (DuFour, 2004). To succeed, we need to be true to the meaning of learning communities.

The kind of simple, powerful practices and structures described here do not always go by the name of "learning communities": Business and industry talk about "self-managing teams," "quality circles," or "team-based organizations" (Peters, 1987). Peter Senge talks about "communities of practice" (1999). In education, we might refer to "continuous improvement teams" or "collaborative communities."

I will refer to all of the above with the terms "learning communities" or "professional learning communities," or PLCs. To be effective, we have to know their essential elements—what they are and are not. We have to be better at telling the real thing from the impostors. And we have to understand why learning communities are a particularly timely and potent force for better schools.

To illustrate how simple the concept is, consider the math department at Johnson City High School in New York. In one year, only 47% of their students passed the New York Regents Competency Exam. Did they decide to invest in a new math text or program or to bring in an outside consultant to conduct a series of workshops? No. Instead, math teachers simply divided the essential skills and knowledge from the Regents Exam into four quarters. They assembled a set of short, quarterly assessments for these topics and then met regularly to help each other prepare, test, and refine the best lessons and strategies they could devise—together rather than individually—to address the most difficult topics. Their common assessments acted as a self-managing mechanism. And—no surprise here—these assessments greatly increased the odds that teachers would teach the essential skills.

But these common, *short-term* assessments also gave teachers something just as essential but rare in the teaching profession: frequent feedback on how well their short-term efforts were succeeding. Without this frequent feedback, improvement was impossible. With it, teachers could make corrections and adjustments when it counted—regularly during the school year. As a result of this simple set of practices, the number of students who succeeded on the New York Regents Exam rose from 47% to 93% in a single year.

Such team-based efforts and their outcomes throughout a school or system are the essence of the professional learning community. This applies to the central office as well. Its practices must both mimic and support such communities in the schools. The use of PLCs is the best, least expensive, most professionally rewarding way to improve schools. In both education and industry, there has been a prolonged, collective cry for such collaborative communities for more than a generation now. Such communities hold out immense, unprecedented hope for schools and the improvement of teaching. A brief look at the history and the current culture of schools will help us fully appreciate this.

The Case for Learning Communities

For his classic 1975 book, *Schoolteacher,* Dan Lortie interviewed hundreds of teachers and found that they worked in almost total isolation relative to other professions. They neither saw nor knew much about their colleagues' practices, and they received almost no feedback on their own practice. Though they were occasionally "evaluated," it became clear that these evaluations were largely perfunctory and intended to create only the facade of constructive supervision (Elmore, 2000). Most of what teachers did on a daily and weekly basis was known only to them. Hence, they received almost no constructive critique on the quality of their instruction. The manifest differences in instructional quality provided by different teachers were not emphasized or acknowledged.

This isolation was so complete that teachers quickly learned that they could teach whatever they liked (or did not like) *however they liked* (Berliner, 1984; Marzano, Marzano, & Pickering, 2003). There was almost no real risk of criticism or consequences. Tenure was virtually guaranteed (Hess, 2004). Unlike other professions, no one would ever monitor either the quality of their work or, very importantly, *its impact on student learning.* Teachers saw that the system readily accommodated even their least effective colleagues, despite the dire consequences this had for generations of students (Marzano, Marzano, & Pickering, 2003; Sanders & Horn, 1994).

The devastating implications of such privacy and isolation were seldom uttered, but were nonetheless quite clear: differences in teaching did not matter much; outcomes were irrelevant until recently.

Teachers were carefully protected from ever having to examine even the most obvious evidence that challenged these assumptions, such as student work or achievement data. Parents and communities never saw this evidence either, as the system successfully managed to "buffer" them from the realities of schooling or from any close outside inspection (Elmore, 2000).

This isolation reflected a profound indifference to instruction and gave teachers tacit, near-total autonomy—permission to teach as well or as poorly as they wished. Curriculum anarchy prevailed. Some teachers taught writing, but most did not. Some classes finished the math text, while others did not even cover half of it (Berliner, 1984; Little, 1990; Marzano, Marzano, & Pickering, 2003). None of this was monitored or corrected.

The Effects of Isolation

Did teachers enjoy this? Yes and no. Many became addicted to this privacy, to working in schools with no supervisory pressure or oversight. For others, such professional privacy led to boredom and professional uncertainty, both of which hobbled any ethos of improvement (Lortie, 1975). Lortie found teachers to be surprisingly "hesitant and uneasy" about the quality of their work and its impact. A sad, numbing fatalism prevailed. Carefully protected from countervailing evidence, they came to regard student outcomes as inevitable, rather than as the result of their deliberate efforts to design and refine instruction. We now know this is a sure recipe for apathy, frustration, and professional stagnation (Csikszentmihalyi, 1990; Evans, 1989).

In such an environment, why would teachers see any value in working closely with colleagues? After all, levels of achievement were largely a result of factors they did not control. Other professions understand that collective efforts to improve, sharpen, and refine one's professional practices have a profound and palpable impact on quality and improvement. In science, industry, medicine, and technology, professional effort and advancement are continuously nourished and accelerated by learning from and working with one's colleagues; collective work and effort are the engine for improvement and a vital source of professional and psychological satisfaction. As Arthur Wise (2004) tells us, "Professionals do not work alone; they work in teams . . . the team delivers the services" (p. 43).

But this has not been the case in education. Numerous researchers have found that teachers were denied the opportunity to clearly see that their efforts could make an enormous, even immediate difference—regardless of the socioeconomic characteristics of their students (Marzano, Marzano, & Pickering, 2003; Mortimore & Sammons, 1987; Sanders & Horn, 1994). In such a system, teacher efficacy and professionalism took a major hit; teachers were not given organized opportunities to study and enjoy the positive effects of their collective thought and effort.

Thus, to a great degree, teaching became a less professional endeavor. Many teachers taught the same lessons from the beginning to the end of their careers, regardless of their impact on learning, and without anyone paying much attention. They were not expected to evaluate or adjust their lessons. As a purely private affair, teaching had become the "not-quite profession" (Darling-Hammond, 1997). Teacher isolation was the central issue here, the very "*enemy of improvement*" (Elmore, 2000).

From Isolation to Collaboration

Isolation is the enemy of improvement. Fortunately, the work of Lortie and others was noted by some members of the educational community. Judith Warren Little was among those who built on these important discoveries. Starting in 1981, she brought the issue of professional privacy to the forefront and exposed improvement's "best friend": the *right kind* of collegiality and collaboration.

Little was tough-minded and nuanced on this topic. Her seminal studies revealed what schools, to this day, most need to acknowledge but have not: that true learning communities—like the one in Johnson City—are characterized by disciplined, professional collaboration and ongoing assessment. This is the surest, most promising route to better school performance, and the reasons are compelling.

Teachers do not learn best from outside experts or by attending conferences or implementing "programs" installed by outsiders. Teachers learn best from other teachers, in settings where they literally teach each other the art of teaching. For this to happen, collaboration had to occur in a radically different way than most of what Little saw. Productive collaboration could not be casual or general; it was instead characterized by:

> Frequent, continuous, and increasingly *concrete* and *precise* talk about teaching practice . . . *adequate to the complexities* of teaching and capable

of *distinguishing one practice and its virtue from another* [italics added]. (Little, 1987, pp. 12–13)

Like Lortie, Little noticed that teachers commonly avoided a focus on the concrete details of effective teaching when they met; they were more comfortable discussing instruction generally and at a distance. This allowed them to talk about instruction without actually having to change it.

Similarly, she found that unless the goals of collaboration were explicitly focused on achievement, the dynamics of team meetings would prevent any meaningful critique of current practice that would lead to improvement; typical teamwork tended to "confirm present practice without evaluating its worth." In such settings, teachers felt comfortable merely "sharing" their work (Little, 1990, p. 517).

But such comfort came at a high price: it precluded the essential recognition of relative differences in quality or accomplishment. Little noted that improvement demanded an overt acknowledgement that some teaching had a greater impact on learning. Indeed, effective leadership required that "the accomplishments of individuals must be recognized and celebrated" (Little, 1987, p. 514). A cascade of other studies— including Gallup polls—have since demonstrated how important this is (Blasé & Kirby, 1992; Buckingham & Coffman, 1999; Nelson, 1994; Peters, 1987). Lortie had noticed a glaring absence of such recognition in schools, which were, if anything, characterized by a "paucity" of recognition and celebration, a "modesty of occasions which produce prideful feelings." This only "underscores the difficulty teachers see in attaining worthwhile results" (Lortie, 1975, p. 133).

These were simple practices:

- Clear, frequent talk about the concrete details of instruction focused on the attainment of explicit achievement goals

- Recognition and celebration of superior practices and their subsequent results

However simple, they ran counter to everything in school culture: the imprecision and ambiguity in many teacher conversations, the failure to talk about the details (for example, the inclusion and execution of certain steps and actions in a lesson plan), and the failure to routinely assess the effectiveness of teaching practices against intended outcomes. These were all simple and sensible practices that were commonly ignored or avoided when teachers collaborated.

Nonetheless, the movement gained ground. Here and there, teachers were willing to abandon generalities and feel-good teacher talk for something with a harder edge—something empirical and precise—and with impressive and consistent results (Schmoker, 1999). They were willing to forego the cheap, easy pleasures of autonomy for the more enduring satisfactions of seeing their collective work pay off concretely *and frequently.*

The "Most Promising Strategy"

The work of Little and her colleagues, like Milbrey McLaughlin and Joan Talbert, eventually revealed the prime importance of this factor in school improvement. These seminal studies and successful schools were building an increasingly iron-clad case for learning communities. Only schools that had "strong teacher communities" could be expected to truly and continuously "re-invent practice" and "advance learning" (McLaughlin & Talbert, 2001). McLaughlin could now write with confidence that:

> The most promising strategy for sustained, substantive school improvement is developing the ability for school personnel to function as professional learning communities. (quoted in DuFour & Eaker, 1998, p. xi)

Despite the still-dismaying shortage of such professional learning communities, their effectiveness cannot be denied: over the years, innumerable and prominent researchers have confirmed their simple power (Schmoker, 2004).

Michael Fullan is among them. One of the keenest observers and synthesizers of educational research, he saw the same power and evidence for learning communities. Starting in the early 1990s, he cited the work of McLaughlin, Talbert, Rosenholtz, Little, and others whose work pointed to the manifold ways in which structured collegiality was richly connected to a litany of benefits—from job satisfaction to "getting results" (Fullan, 1991).

He was emphatic about this connection, writing that "no words could sum up" the best we know about school improvement better than Little's: "School improvement is most surely and thoroughly achieved" when teachers engage in the kind of collaboration we have described here (Fullan, 1991, p. 78).

Fullan's work is important for another reason: he was one of the first to break ranks with many of his colleagues to note the vital resonance between studies in education and industry. This link reinforced the emerging knowledge from Little and others and represented a common pattern in another field.

The Link With Industry

The parallel developments in business and industry gave added strength and credence to the case for team-based learning communities. In 1982, Tom Peters and Robert Waterman made business publishing history with their blockbuster bestseller *In Search of Excellence*. Here and in subsequent publications, Peters stressed the same essential features of effective teams: an insistence on frequent, tightly-focused, collective effort; on measurement that could guide and refine this short-term effort, and on "unprecedented celebration and recognition" of even the smallest improvements and their impact on short-term results (hugely important for Peters). Peters' books abounded in illustrative cases; the evidence for disciplined teams was so strong that he could assert that "the self-managing team should become *the basic organizational building block*" [italics added] (1987, p. 297).

The application of these simple assertions was exceedingly successful in many large and small organizations. These assertions also established the context for what Peters called a "management revolution" (Peters, 1987). They changed everything in most industries—but not yet in education.

Redefining Leadership: The "Self-Managing Team"

Team-based structures also have enormous and positive implications for leadership. The team-based organization would be less expensive and less time-consuming and would probably *reduce or eliminate* the need for close, cumbersome supervision and inspection, which is always problematic (Peters, 1987).

Peters' work was influenced by the work of W. Edwards Deming. The core of Demings' legacy has had significant influence in schools as well as in industry through his call for "self-managing teams." His work demonstrated that productivity is not a function of "mass inspection"—what Peters called "close, front-line supervision" (Peters, 1987, p. 300). Deming found the widely distributed leadership and shared responsibility of self-managing teams generated better results with less supervision.

Talent and sustained commitment are most apt to flourish in team settings that:

1. Combine autonomy *and* responsibility for results, and

2. Provide abundant opportunities for individuals to share their collective and complementary skills and abilities toward better results.

An important discovery was made: such collective but autonomous effort brought out the best in people. What Little called "collective autonomy" will always achieve better results than individuals working under close, rigid supervision. Little wrote that significant improvement "cannot be accomplished by even the most knowledgeable individuals working alone" (1990, p. 520) because teaching is so complex. Similarly, Deming wrote that there was "no substitute for teamwork, without which we have dissipation of knowledge and effort, results far from optimum" (1986, p. 19). These ideas spread and took root throughout business and industry. In 1992, Peter Senge could say at the American Association of School Administrators' conference that "there probably isn't a Fortune

500 company that isn't doing Deming." It is a testament to the power of self-managing teams that the vast majority of productive companies have embraced these methods, even if they do not know their source.

A turning point in education could be seen in a landmark article in *Educational Leadership.* In "The Learning Principal," Rick DuFour (2002) made the case for a new kind of leadership. He spoke for those administrators whose attempts to become the consummate "instructional leader" by attempting to "mass inspect" every aspect of instruction had ended in frustration. He found that his time and effort had far more impact when primarily focused on *learning*—on assessment results—rather than on instruction. This indicates an interesting shift from "instructional leader" to "learning leader." The leader's function is to provide opportunities for teachers to work together in self-managing teams to improve *their own* instruction, always with the expectation for improved learning. The principal's job is to monitor, discuss, and support teachers' progress in achieving higher levels of student *learning* on both short-term and annual assessments. This is the best use of his or her valuable time.

This radical shift could only occur with the emergence of another important and radical discovery that employees—teachers—largely know how to improve their own instruction or can work in teams to figure it out together.

The Knowing-Doing Gap

Another discovery that points to the timeliness and power of professional learning communities is the emergent realization that training, though useful, is overrated and, in some cases, even unnecessary (Berliner, 1984; Fullan quoted in Sparks, 2003a). The old and failed model insisted that "staff development" was the primary source of productive knowledge and practice.

Dennis Sparks is the executive director of the National Staff Development Council and one of my favorite conduits of original insights, important books, and trends. He once told me that he was convinced that any faculty, with no additional formal training or professional development, already had enough practical knowledge and ability to make continuous and significant improvements to instruction.

I thought about what he said for a few days and realized that he was right. The problem is not that we do not know enough—it is that we do not *do what we already know*. We do not act on or refine or apply those principles and practices that *virtually every teacher already knows*.

Here are some telling examples: I have asked teachers in small and large groups if they own or have access to rubrics. They do, and they acknowledge the proven importance of rubrics. Then they admit, in overwhelming numbers, that very few teachers even use rubrics, much less actually teach students their meaning or how to use them to self-assess their work before handing it in, which is precisely the rubric's purpose and function.

Most teachers agree with me that purposeful reading for higher-order or analytical purposes is essential and should occur daily. Then they admit, in droves, that it rarely occurs in their classrooms. They admit that writing is crucial to intellectual development, but then admit (as research clearly confirms) that students do very little meaningful writing in American classrooms (Allington, 2001). They know that "modeling," where teachers carefully demonstrate skill or thought processes out loud and explicitly, is a "make-or-break" element in an effective lesson. But they indicate that very little effective modeling is ever even attempted or included in most of their lesson plans. Teachers even confirm what I have observed in hundreds of classrooms: many, many lessons do not include any assessment component. The lessons are only instructional activities that are wrongly considered to be effective or aligned with important learning skills and standards (Schmoker, 2001). With the exception of a few teachers, the education of my own children in three different schools confirms these findings.

That teachers have not acted on what they know indicates the presence of a knowing-doing gap in their practice. The problem is not that we do not *know* what to do—it is that we do not *do* what we know. When Peter Block was interviewed by Dennis Sparks, he noted that in most industries and professions, people *think* they need more training. In fact, "we have all the skills, the tools, the training we need" (Sparks, 2003b, p. 52). What we need is to work in teams to apply what we know and support each other as we implement and refine implementation. In the *Knowing-Doing Gap*, Pfeffer and Sutton (2000) tell us that successful organizations—such as Honda and Toyota—learn from each other, in teams, how to capitalize on expertise that they already possess. Such organizations found that success depends largely on *implementing what is already known* rather than on adopting new or previously unknown ways of doing things.

My visit to the Toyota plant in Georgetown, Kentucky, forcefully confirms this (Schmoker & Wilson, 1992). It is not, as Jim Collins writes in *Good to Great*, the big initiatives or new large-scale discoveries that promote productivity; it is a simple focus on refining processes in small but innumerable ways

(2001). Such small but powerful adjustments emerge in team settings where a desire for improvement is encouraged by collective reinforcement and ongoing recognition and celebration of each small step forward until, as Collins puts it, the essential positive "momentum" is achieved.

Can we afford to go on ignoring such a preponderance of knowledge and evidence that so clearly indicates the need for self-managing professional learning communities? How much longer will our professional integrity allow us to indulge in the fantasy that we are doing the best we can to improve schools, despite the manifest evidence that our best weapon against mediocrity and academic inequity has not even been given a fighting chance?

We can close the gap—right now—between what we know and what we do with learning communities. The benefits for students and for education professionals will be incalculable. So let's get on with it.

References

Allington, R. A. (2001). *What really matters for struggling readers.* New York: Longman.

Berliner, D. (1984). The glass half-full: A review of research on teaching. In P. J. Hosford (Ed.), *Using what we know about teaching.* Alexandria, VA: Association of Supervision and Curriculum Development.

Blasé, J., & Kirby, P. C. (1992, December). The power of praise—A strategy for effective schools. *NASSP Bulletin, 76,* 69–77.

Buckingham, M., & Coffman, C. (1999). *First break all the rules.* New York: Simon and Schuster.

Collins, J. (2001). *Good to great.* New York: Harper Business.

Csikszentmihalyi, M. (1990). *Flow: The psychology of optimal experience.* New York: Harper Perrenial.

Darling-Hammond, L. (1997). *The right to learn: A blueprint for creating schools that work.* New York: Jossey-Bass.

Deming, W. E. (1986). *Out of the crisis.* Cambridge, MA: MIT Press.

DuFour, R. (2002). The learning principal. *Educational Leadership, 59*(8), 12–15.

DuFour, R. (2004). What is a professional learning community? *Educational Leadership, 61*(8), 6–11.

DuFour, R., & Eaker, R. (1998). *Professional learning communities at work: Best practices for enhancing student achievement.* Bloomington, IN: Solution Tree (formerly National Educational Service).

Elmore, R. (2000). *Building a new structure for school leadership.* Washington, DC: Albert Shanker Institute.

Evans, R. (1989). The faculty in midcareer: Implications for school improvement. *Educational Leadership, 51*(1), 19–23.

Fullan, M. G., with Stiegelbauer, S. (1991). *The new meaning of educational change.* New York: Teacher's College Press.

Hess, F. (2004). *Common sense school reform.* New York: Palgrave McMillan.

Little, J. W. (1987). Teachers as colleagues. In V. Richardson-Koehler (Ed.), *Educators Handbook.* White Plains, NY: Longman.

Little, J. W. (1990). The persistence of privacy: Autonomy and initiative in teachers' professional relations. *Teachers' College Record, 91*(4), 509–536.

Lortie, D. (1975). *Schoolteacher: A sociological study.* Chicago: University of Chicago Press.

Marzano, R., Marzano, J., & Pickering. D. (2003). *Classroom management that works.* Alexandria, VA: Association of Supervision and Curriculum Development.

McLaughlin, M. W., & Talbert, J. E. (2001). *Professional communities and the work of high school teaching.* Chicago: University of Chicago Press.

Mortimore, P., & Sammons, P. (1987). New evidence on effective elementary schools. *Educational Leadership, 45*(1), 4–8.

Nelson, B. (1994). *1001 ways to reward employees.* New York: Workman.

Peters, T. (1987). *Thriving on chaos.* New York: Alfred A. Knopf.

Peters, T., & Waterman, R. (1982). *In search of excellence.* New York: Harper and Row.

Pfeffer, J., & Sutton, R. I. (2000). *The knowing-doing gap: How smart companies turn knowledge into action.* Boston: Allyn and Bacon.

Sanders, W. L., & Horn, S. P. (1994). The Tennessee Value-Added Assessment System (TVASS): Mixed-model methodology in educational assessment. *Journal of Personnel Evaluation in Education, 8,* 299–311.

Schmoker, M. (1999). *Results: The key to continuous school improvement* (2nd ed.). Alexandria, VA: Association of Supervision and Curriculum Development.

Schmoker, M. (2001, October 24). The Crayola curriculum. *Education Week, 21,* p. 8.

Schmoker, M. (2004). Tipping point: From feckless reform to substantive instructional improvement. *Phi Delta Kappan, 85*(6), 424–432.

Schmoker, M., & Wilson, R. B. (1992, January). Quest for quality. *The Executive Educator, 17*(4), 18–24.

Senge, P. M. (1992, February 24). From a speech presented at the annual conference of the American Association for School Administrators in San Diego, CA.

Senge, P. M. (1999). Leadership in living organizations. In *Leading beyond the walls,* pp. 1–11. San Francisco: Jossey-Bass.

Sparks, D. (2003a). Change agent: An interview with Michael Fullan. *Journal of Staff Development, 24*(1), 55–58.

Sparks, D. (2003b). The answer to when is now: An interview with Peter Block. *Journal of Staff Development, 24*(2), 52–56.

Sparks, D. (2004). From hunger aid to school reform. *Journal of Staff Development, 25*(1), 46–51.

Wise, A. (2004). Teaching teams: A 21st Century paradigm for organizing America's schools. *Education Week, 24*(5), 43.

Dennis Sparks

Dr. Dennis Sparks has been described as "the voice of professional development in the United States." As the executive director of the 10,000 member National Staff Development Council, Dr. Sparks has been a forceful advocate for job-embedded staff development, arguing that schools should be organized into professional learning communities in which staff members learn from one another as part of their routine work practices. He contributes to each issue of the *Journal of Staff Development* as a columnist and is the author of the recently published *Leading for Results: Transforming Teaching, Learning, and Relationships in Schools.* He is also author of *Designing Powerful Professional Development for Teachers and Principals; Conversations That Matter; Learning to Lead, Leading to Learn; What Is Staff Development Anyway?* and *A New Vision for Staff Development.*

In this chapter, Dr. Sparks links high-quality professional learning to successful professional learning communities. He cites three formidable barriers schools must overcome if they are to develop as PLCs: lack of clarity regarding values, intentions, and beliefs; dependence on those outside of the schools for solutions to problems; and a sense of resignation that robs educators of the energy that is essential to the continuous improvement of teaching, learning, and relationships in school. He contends that effective leadership is essential to overcoming these barriers, and he offers a definition of leadership that goes far beyond traditional hierarchical positions.

He notes that "at their essence professional learning communities are places in which everyone is both a teacher and a student." He suggests that great leaders must be great teachers, and he calls upon all leaders to shape the culture of their schools by developing and communicating "Teachable Points of View" through stories and dialogue.

Dr. Dennis Sparks' interviews and articles are accessible on the NSDC web site at www.nsdc.org/library/authors/sparks.cfm.

Chapter 8

Leading for Transformation in Teaching, Learning, and Relationships

Dennis Sparks

My work in the field of staff development for the past 25 years has revealed to me the deep feelings of discontent among countless teachers, administrators, and policy makers regarding the quality of professional learning in schools. Many educational leaders from the schoolhouse to the statehouse are frustrated with the glacially slow pace of change in this critically important area.

The positive side of such frustration, though, is the energy it generates for deep and significant change in professional learning in schools and a recognition at all levels that if we continue to do what we have always done, we will get what we have always gotten. Leaders are challenging entrenched thinking about staff development practices that for far too long have ill-served teachers and their students.

Readers of this book probably know better than anyone that high-quality professional learning is essential if school reform efforts are to truly improve the quality of teaching and learning in schools. Successful professional learning communities clearly demonstrate what is possible when teachers learn and collaborate within their schools as part of their daily work. Well-implemented professional learning communities are a powerful means of seamlessly blending teaching and professional learning in ways that produce complex, intelligent behavior in all teachers.

David Perkins (2004) lists four "knowledge arts" that he would like schools to cultivate in students that are in tune with the goals of professional learning communities:

- Creating knowledge
- Communicating knowledge
- Organizing knowledge
- Acting on knowledge

Professional learning communities extend these knowledge arts to teachers: teachers create knowledge about teaching and learning, communicate it to one another, organize it within themselves and for others to make it more meaningful and accessible, and act on that knowledge for the purpose of improving student learning.

Leaders Matter

Leaders matter in the creation and long-term maintenance of professional learning communities. The quality of teaching, learning, and relationships in professional learning communities depends on the quality of leadership provided by principals and teachers. I contend that by the very fact that you are reading this book, you are a leader no matter what your position. I also contend that leaders matter because they have the authority to shape conversations—what is talked about and how it is talked about—through "Teachable Points of View" and "Interactive Teaching" (terms I will explain later) that lead to essential professional learning. Leaders shape conversations by persistently offering their values, intentions, and beliefs to others and by expressing themselves in clear declarative sentences. Leaders also matter because they, along with others, shape a school or school system's structure and culture in ways that promote learning, collaboration, and environments in which all members of the community feel cared for and respected.

Profound change in schools, I believe, begins with profound change in leaders, which radiates out to others and into the "system." Structural change is almost always required, but it is not sufficient. New positions can be created, job descriptions rewritten, and teaching schedules modified—to name just a few structural changes—without deeply affecting teachers' understanding of what they teach, the ways in which they teach it, or their relationships with one another and with their students.

Profound change in leaders results from and is revealed through deeper understanding of complex issues related to professional learning communities, beliefs that are aligned with quality teaching and high levels of learning for all students, and "next action thinking" that moves learning into action and sustains the momentum of change over time. As a result of their professional learning, leaders alter what they think, say, and do in ways that are observable to others. Put another way, profound professional learning produces teachers and administrators who say what they have not said, believe what they have not believed, understand what they have not understood, and do what they have not done. Without change in those vital areas, I believe that very little of substance will change in ways that improve teaching and student learning.

This chapter will describe how leaders can alter what they think, say, and do to address what I believe are the most fundamental barriers to professional learning communities so that what I have termed the "final two percent" of professional learning occurs. The primary means for leaders' ongoing learning, as I will explain later, is their development of Teachable Points of View and their engagement of members of the school community in dialogue regarding their views.

The "Final Two Percent"

Of all the things that are said and done at the national, state, and local level to improve the quality of professional learning and collaboration in schools, only a handful directly affect what teachers learn and how well they work together. Imagine a set of events and activities along a continuum that leads to high-quality professional learning that improves teaching and increases student achievement. On the left side of the continuum are federal, state, and district policies and regulations that are intended to affect professional development. In the middle of the continuum are structural changes and planning decisions regarding school improvement goals, strategies, and evaluation processes. All of these activities— state and federal legislation, board and administrative policies, structural changes, the reallocation of resources, and district and school improvement planning, to name a few—are merely preludes to the activities that actually produce the professional learning (knowledge, skills, beliefs), collaborative relationships, and improved practice that are their intended goal. Expressed another way, while schools may declare themselves professional learning communities, alter their schedules to enable teams of teachers to meet on a regular basis, and allocate resources to teacher leadership positions such as mentors or academic coaches, these activities are insufficient unless the final two percent of activities are carefully considered and well executed on a day-to-day basis.

The final two percent is that cluster of experiences that literally change the brains of teachers and administrators. Educators have these experiences when they read, write, observe, use various thinking strategies, listen, speak, and practice new behaviors in ways that deepen understanding, affect beliefs, produce new habits of mind and behavior, and are combined in ways that alter practice. Such professional learning produces complex, intelligent behavior in all teachers and leaders and continuously enhances their professional judgment.

The professional learning activities themselves that comprise the final two percent can take many forms, some familiar and others less familiar to most teachers. The more familiar forms are designed a lot like a classroom—someone (a teacher, administrator, professor, or consultant) teaches teachers in a group setting. Optimally, this design uses methods that align with the school or school system's sense of "good teaching."

For instance, Paul Black, Christine Harrison, Clare Lee, Bethan Marshall, and Dylan Wiliam (2004) offer their view of effective teaching by describing generic teaching strategies that if consistently applied "would raise a school in the lower quartile of the national performance tables to well above average" (p. 11).

They mention procedures such as:

- Allowing longer wait time to encourage students to move from brief, factual answers to extended statements and to engage more students in discussions

- Providing students with comments on written and oral responses rather than through numerical scores or letter grades

- Using peer and self assessment to promote deeper learning

Teachers who learned about these research findings, the authors report,

> . . . built up a repertoire of generic skills. They planned their questions, allowed appropriate wait time, and gave feedback that was designed to cause thinking. They ensured that students were given enough time during lessons to evaluate their own work and that of others. (p. 16)

Drawing on the perspectives offered by other types of research, Jacqueline Grennon Brooks (2004) cites cognitive science and neuropsychological brain studies as a source of guidance on deepening student understanding and increasing motivation. She recommends practices such as seeking and valuing student points of view, 1-minute writing exercises for students to increase their conceptual understanding, and problem-based learning and visual mapping approaches to provide pictorial representations of ideas, objects, and/or events.

It simply makes sense that teachers who learn through approaches such as those recommended by Black and his colleagues and by Brooks are more likely to understand and apply what they have learned. Of particular interest given this book's focus on professional learning communities is Black and his colleagues' conclusion that if these strategies are to be implemented in classrooms it is essential that leaders find time for groups of teachers to meet on a regular basis for study and discussion and for those groups to report on their progress at faculty meetings.

The less familiar final two percent of professional learning activities are especially well suited to the purposes and structures of professional learning communities. *Powerful Designs for Professional Learning* (Easton, 2004) describes a number of such methods: action research, designing and evaluation of student assessments, case discussions, classroom walk-throughs, critical friends groups, curriculum design, data analysis, lesson study, journal writing, mentoring, peer coaching, portfolios, shadowing students, tuning protocols, and study groups, to name a few. This type of staff development "is *powerful* because it arises from and returns to the world of teaching and learning," Easton writes. "It begins with what will really help young people learn, engages those involved in helping them learn, and has an effect on the classrooms (and schools, districts, even states) where those students and their teachers learn" (p. 2).

The final two percent also includes the culture-shaping activities that affect what is discussed by teachers, the manner in which it is discussed, the openness with which group members offer and absorb various perspectives, and the energy generated by connections to a worthy purpose and to respected colleagues (Sparks, 2005). These activities address the interpersonal challenges of leadership, the unpredictable and emotionally laden experiences that have a significant effect on human performance and relationships.

Fundamental Barriers to Professional Learning Communities

When educators discuss barriers to professional community in schools, they almost always mention lack of money and time, recalcitrant teachers or teacher unions, and principals and district administrators who lack desire or skill in leading such efforts. While most schools would benefit from additional resources, particularly those schools serving high concentrations of low-income and minority students, few schools effectively use the professional learning resources currently available to them. For example, faculty, department, and grade-level meetings are seldom used to promote learning and meaningful collaboration regarding teaching and learning. Staff development days often lack focus, substance, continuity across time, and extension into classroom practice in ways that significantly affect teaching. Given that perspective, I believe the primary barriers to professional learning communities are:

- A lack of clarity regarding values, intentions, and beliefs

- Dependence on those outside of the school for solutions to problems

- A sense of resignation that robs educators of the energy that is essential to the continuous improvement of teaching, learning, and relationships in schools

The importance of **clarity** is based on the premises that we move toward what is clearest to us and that it is very difficult to create what we cannot describe in some detail. Fortunately, we have the ability to clarify our values, intentions, and beliefs through processes such as writing and discussion with others.

Dependence means that teachers and principals wait for others to direct their actions. It is a byproduct of school reform initiatives that the source of direction and knowledge resides outside of K–12 schools in the hands of policymakers, researchers, and consultants. Schools are more likely to thrive, I believe, when they function interdependently with district offices, universities, and other educational entities. Schools can benefit from knowledge and perspectives derived from the outside, but for many schools the balance between internal and external sources of knowledge and action has become so skewed that those in schools no longer see themselves as initiators of action or inventors of solutions to problems.

Mike Schmoker (2004) notes the prevalence of these particular barriers when he argues that "clarity precedes competence" (p. 85) and that failure in professional learning communities often stems from confusion about fundamental concepts, including what is meant by "collaboration." Schmoker laments the culture of dependency in schools, observing that "I routinely encounter teachers and administrators who are waiting, endlessly, needlessly, for the right research or staff development programs" (p. 87).

Resignation is an intellectual and emotional state in which educators believe that their individual and collective actions cannot improve teaching and learning, particularly given the large and serious problems that affect the lives of far too many students and their families. A profound consequence of this belief is that teachers and administrators act as if they have a very small, or perhaps even nonexistent, circle of influence related to student learning.

Here is an example from my recent experience: A teacher friend described an "in-service" in which an elementary school faculty watched videotapes about professional learning communities. My friend commented that the person speaking in the video, who happened to be Rick DuFour, said that there are obstacles to the development of professional learning communities and that she wished he had said what they were. I responded that I believed that the faculty of her school could do a pretty good job in an hour or two of identifying the barriers that stood in their way and that the list would be at least as helpful as any that Rick might have provided. She doubted that was true, and our conversation eventually turned to other things.

The good news is that each of us as leaders can do something about those problems, starting with ourselves. We extend our influence on teaching, learning, and relationships within schools when we are clear about our values, intentions, and assumptions. We also extend our influence when we act in ways that are consistent with the belief that we already possess the ability and authority to improve teaching, learning, and relationships.

A "Teachable Point of View"

At their essence, successful professional learning communities are places in which everyone is both a teacher and a student. Continuous improvement in teaching, student achievement, and the quality of relationships among all members of the community is based on a continuous cycle of teaching and learning and an openness by everyone in the community to learn from everyone else in the community—no matter what their title or status.

In *The Cycles of Leadership: How Great Leaders Teach Their Companies to Win*, Noel Tichy (2002) describes the leader's role in such organizations: "Teaching is the most effective means through which a leader can lead" (p. 57). He adds:

> Everyone in the organization is expected to be constantly in a teaching and learning mode. . . . True learning takes place only when the leader/teacher invests the time and emotional energy to engage those around him or her in a dialogue that produces mutual understanding. (p. 58)

The starting point, Tichy says, is when "a leader commits to teaching, creates the conditions for being taught him or herself, and helps the students have the self confidence to engage and teach as well" (p. 21).

This teaching and learning is enacted, Tichy says, through Virtuous Teaching Cycles in which learning flows in various directions throughout the organization. Leaders' Teachable Points of View (TPOVs) provide the content, and interactive teaching offers the means for the learning. "In a Virtuous Teaching Cycle," Tichy writes, "each act or event of teaching improves the knowledge and abilities of both the students and the teachers and spurs them both to go on and share what they have learned with others. It creates a cascade of teaching and learning" (pp. 52–53).

A TPOV, Tichy writes, is "a cohesive set of ideas and concepts that a person is able to articulate clearly to others" (p. 74). A TPOV reveals clarity of thought regarding ideas and values and is a tool for communicating them to others, he says. Tichy believes it is critical that leaders have TPOVs about an "urgent need that is clear and palpable to everyone in the organization" (p. 85), "a mission that is inspiring and clearly worth achieving" (p. 86), "goals that stretch people's abilities"

(p. 86), and "a spirit of teamwork" (p. 88). He also recommends that leaders develop TPOVs for the central ideas that will move the organization toward its goals, on the values that express the type of behavior desired by the organization, on the ways to generate positive emotional energy within the organization, and on the "edge"—the thought processes that inform tough yes or no decisions.

Creating Teachable Points of View

Earlier in this chapter, I asserted that significant change in organizations begins with significant change in what leaders think, say, and do. I also claimed that as this change radiates out to others it can have a profound effect on the quality of professional learning within a school and ultimately on the school's culture and structures. These changes, I believe, have their origins in clarity regarding ideas, values, intentions, assumptions, requests, and next actions. That clarity is best expressed in simple, declarative sentences. In my experience, it is very difficult to accomplish things we cannot describe. Teachable Points of View of various lengths and levels of complexity prepared in different language and forms for different audiences and time frames provide an ideal means for achieving such clarity.

"The very act of creating a Teachable Point of View makes people better leaders," Tichy argues. "Leaders come to understand their underlying assumptions about themselves, their organization, and business in general. When implicit knowledge becomes explicit, it can then be questioned, refined, and honed, which benefits both the leaders and the organizations" (p. 97).

Creating a TPOV is an unfamiliar and challenging task for many leaders, Tichy recognizes. "It requires first doing the intellectual work of figuring out what our point of view is, and then the creative work of putting it into a form that makes it accessible and interesting to others" (p. 100).

Creating a TPOV is hard work, Tichy acknowledges:

> It requires a total commitment of head, heart, and guts. The head part is the intellectual work of taking decades of implicit internal knowledge and making it explicit. . . . It means framing the various ideas and beliefs that underlie your actions, and then tying them together into a cohesive whole. (p. 101)

Tichy strongly recommends writing as a means of developing a TPOV. In addition, he recommends reflecting, getting feedback from others, and revising: "The process of articulating one's Teachable Point of View is not a one-time event. It is an ongoing, iterative and interactive process" (p. 103). Marge Scherer (2004) warns that "writing well will always be one of the toughest and one of the most rewarding endeavors a human being can undertake. Good writing involves clear thinking, originality, cogent arguments, and compelling examples" (p. 7).

A starting place in the creation of TPOVs is for leaders to write a few hundred words on one of the topics suggested above by Tichy or on a wide variety of subjects of importance within professional learning communities. For instance, leaders might create TPOVs related to professional learning and collaboration in their schools, instructional leadership, quality teaching, the attributes of the relationships desired in the school among teachers and between teachers and students, and various means of assessing student progress in addition to standardized tests.

Or leaders might take the advice offered by Dennis Littky in *The Big Picture: Education Is Everyone's Business* (2004):

> Start right now by creating your own vision of how your school might become a great school. Start this as an internal dialogue, use the margins of this book or a journal to sketch out your first ideas, and then get together with people around you and begin to build a collective vision. Imagine what your school would look like if the changes you imagine began to take hold. Live off that beauty and let it push you on. (p. 195)

I encourage leaders to develop TPOVs on important subjects that vary in length from 5-minute "vision speeches" to day-long interactive teaching events to brief presentations for faculty meetings, parent get-togethers, and other venues that promote the type of learning processes proposed in the following section. Leaders can also gather a school's leadership team and create common TPOVs around central ideas and values.

The boxed feature on pages 169 and 170 shows an example of a Teachable Point of View based on my own experiences that I might use at a staff meeting if I were a principal of a school. Over time, a principal might create additional TPOVs for each of the italicized words or phrases in the sample. The TPOVs would be of different lengths and levels of complexity depending on the purpose (to inform the school community, to engage teachers in dialogue on important issues, and so on) and the audience (teachers, parents, or students). They might be spoken or distributed in written form through newsletters, web sites, or other means of communication. With experience, leaders

Sample Teachable Point of View

I believe that the quality of our teaching is the most important thing in determining the quality of learning that students experience in this school. I believe that the quality of relationships that we as adults have with each other has a profound effect on the quality of relationships students experience here, both with us and with other students. I want every student to experience *quality teaching* in every classroom and be surrounded and supported by *quality relationships* with adults and peers.

The data we have been reviewing tell us that we are not yet there, but I believe that we can become such a school if we work together and learn our way into new understandings and practices.

It may be helpful for me to be more specific about a few of my beliefs related to teaching and learning. I believe that *beginning teachers benefit from the practical, day-to-day support of other teachers*. I believe that *the most powerful forms of professional learning occur as part of what teachers do every day* rather than what happens separate from it. The daily tasks of teaching—planning lessons, figuring out how to reach and teach hard-to-teach kids, and communicating with parents, to name a few—are sources of vital teamwork and continuous learning for teachers.

I believe these things in part because of the professional literature we have been studying together over the past year. I also hold these beliefs because as a beginning teacher I had the good fortune to work at a high school in which I was assigned to two teaching teams that met several times a week. We planned our lessons together and watched one another teach. We gave each other feedback, although it was of the most rudimentary form. In addition, the school provided a mentor to guide me during my first year in the classroom.

While I am grateful for those experiences, in retrospect I know that they could have been even more powerful. My teaching colleagues and I did not have a very extensive *intellectual framework or vocabulary to*

(continued)

> **Sample Teachable Point of View** (continued)
>
> *talk about our teaching* so we did not always know how to describe what we were doing and how to improve it. We did not know about *rubrics* and missed the insights they would have provided regarding the quality of student work and the guidance they would have offered us and our students. We did not have any *sources of data* or *other evidence of student learning* beyond scores on teacher-made tests and student papers. My *mentor*, while well intentioned, was not clear about his responsibilities, and because he had not been trained for this role, I floundered more than was necessary.
>
> We are on the right track. We already use several types of data to determine our school and team goals and to measure progress. We have formed ourselves into teams, have developed rubrics that we use with our students, and apply *research on effective teaching* in various subject areas to help us talk to one another about good teaching. To inform our planning we have been reading about mentoring, lesson study, and using *protocols* to inform our discussions of student work. I am confident we can use all of these tools and others to find even better ways to serve our students and one another.

would create more nuanced and complex TPOVs reflecting a wide variety of important subjects.

Using Stories and Dialogue to Convey Teachable Points of View

Leaders communicate their TPOVs through what Tichy calls "interactive teaching." Leaders who engage in interactive teaching operate from the mind-set that they have something to learn from their students as well as something to teach them and that to relate to them in that spirit is more effective than "telling" or "selling."

Stories provide a powerful means by which TPOVs can be explained, illustrated, and understood in human terms. Stories provide listeners with a plot line and a cast of characters. Tichy recommends weaving TPOVs into stories "that people can understand, relate to, and remember. It is not enough to have slogans and mission/values statements. People don't sign up for that. People follow leaders who can make them part of something exciting" (p. 121). Tichy describes three types of stories:

- Who am I? (explains the real-life experiences that have shaped the leader and his or her TPOVs)

- Who are we? (describes the common experiences and beliefs of those in the organization)

- Where are we going? (describes what the organization is aiming to do and how it is going to do it)

Dialogue is another effective means for creating Virtuous Teaching Cycles. Dialogue is distinct from discussion, debate, and argument. Advocacy for a point of view is not part of dialogue, nor does it attempt to convince others that they are wrong. While these methods sometimes have their place, they often produce defensiveness, which is a barrier to the deep understanding and transformational learning that often accompanies dialogue. The assumptions leaders hold as unquestionable truths often represent some of the most fruitful areas for dialogue because alterations in these assumptions can produce profound changes in behavior and relationships. When leaders listen with their full attention and truly honor a speaker's views and experience, relationships are deepened and individuals are profoundly changed.

"Dialogue . . . imposes a rigorous discipline on the participants," Daniel Yankelovich writes in *The Magic of Dialogue: Transforming Conflict Into Cooperation* (1999):

When dialogue is done skillfully, the results can be extraordinary: long standing stereotypes dissolved, mistrust overcome, mutual understanding achieved, visions shaped and grounded in shared purpose, people previously at odds with one another aligned on objectives and strategies, new common ground discovered, new perspectives and insights gained, new levels of creativity stimulated, and bonds of community strengthened. (p. 16)

The discipline that Yankelovich recommends includes equality among participants, an absence of coercive influences, listening with empathy, and bringing assumptions into the open while suspending judgment.

In *Dialogue: Rediscover the Transforming Power of Conversation*, Linda Ellinor and Glenna Gerard (1998) list several qualities of genuine dialogue:

- Suspension of judgment
- Release of our need for a specific outcome
- Inquiry into and examination of underlying assumptions
- Authenticity
- A slower pace of interaction with silence between speakers
- Listening deeply to self and others for collective meaning

To those ends, they suggest:

- Focusing on shared meaning and learning
- Listening without resistance

- Respecting differences

- Suspending role and status distinctions

- Sharing responsibility and leadership

- Speaking to the group as a whole (One-on-one conversations in front of a group can lead to the disengagement of other group members.)

Recommendations

- Focus your professional learning on transforming what you think, say, and do. Translate learning into action. Use transformation in thought, word, and deed as the standard against which you assess the quality of your own learning and that of others in the school community.

- Begin to address lack of clarity, resignation, and dependency by developing Teachable Points of View that address some or all of the topics suggested in this chapter.

- Use various modes of interactive teaching—particularly dialogue—to activate and sustain learning throughout the organization. Engage others in dialogue regarding your TPOVs. Focus on assumptions, ideas, and values. Honor others' views and be open to having your views changed.

- Focus efforts on activities that represent the final two percent of professional learning—the part that literally changes human brains—and collaboration to ensure that teaching, student learning, and relationships are significantly improved.

Skillful leadership on the part of principals and teachers is essential if professional learning communities are to fulfill their primary function of continuously improving the quality of teaching, learning, and relationships in schools. To that end, what leaders think, say, and do matters.

Skillful leaders address the barriers of resignation, dependence, and lack of clarity by clearly articulating their Teachable Points of View through stories and other means, engaging the school community in continuous dialogue regarding their views, and consistently asserting that the potential of students and staff alike can be more fully realized. From my perspective, there is no higher purpose for the exercise of leadership in schools.

References

Black, P., Harrison, C., Lee, C., Marshall, B., & Wiliam, D. (2004). Working inside the black box: Assessment for learning in the classroom. *Phi Delta Kappan, 86*(1), 9–21.

Brooks, J. G. (2004). To see beyond the lesson. *Educational Leadership, 62*(1), 8–12.

Easton, L. (Ed.). (2004). *Powerful designs for professional learning.* Oxford, OH: National Staff Development Council.

Ellinor, L., & Gerard, G. (1998). *Dialogue: Rediscover the transforming power of conversation.* New York: John Wiley & Sons.

Littky, D., with Grabelle, S. (2004). *The big picture: Education is everyone's business.* Alexandria, VA: Association for Supervision and Curriculum Development.

Perkins, D. (2004). Knowledge alive. *Educational Leadership, 62*(1), 14–18.

Scherer, M. (2004). Dream come true? *Educational Leadership, 62*(2), 7.

Schmoker, M. (2004). Learning communities at the crossroads: Toward the best schools we've ever had. *Phi Delta Kappan, 86*(1), 84–88.

Sparks, D. (2005). *Leading for results: Transforming teaching, learning, and relationships in schools.* Thousand Oaks, CA: Corwin Press.

Tichy, N. (2002). *The cycles of leadership: How great leaders teach their companies to win.* New York: Harper Business.

Yankelovich, D. (1999). *The magic of dialogue: Transforming conflict into cooperation.* New York: Simon & Schuster.

Lawrence W. Lezotte

Anyone interested in school improvement is indebted to Dr. Larry Lezotte, an educator whose name has become synonymous with the Effective Schools movement. His pioneering research with Wilbur Brookover was among the first that identified the differences between schools that were effective and improving versus their counterparts that were low-achieving and declining. This research, along with the findings of Ron Edmonds, Michael Rutter, and others, provided compelling evidence that certain aspects of school culture and practice have a significant impact on the academic performance of students.

In addition to his contributions as a researcher, Dr. Lezotte has authored numerous important articles and books, including *Assembly Required: A Continuous School Improvement System* and its companion *Implementation Guide; Learning for All; The Effective Schools Process: A Proven Path to Learning for All; Creating the Total Quality Effective School;* and *Sustainable School Reform: The District Context for School Improvement.* Additionally, he has published a collection of monographs on the Correlates of Effective Schools.

In this chapter, Dr. Lezotte provides a brief background on the history of the Effective Schools research and describes the rationale and processes needed to embed the Effective Schools research in a school improvement process. He asserts that when educators engage in continuous school improvement processes based on this research, they are demonstrating professional learning communities in action.

Many schools that are moving towards functioning as professional learning communities have found that gaining shared knowledge of the Effective Schools research is helpful in developing the school's vision of the future. Analysis of what is known about highly effective schools lays a foundation that can prove very helpful as the faculty more clearly describes the school they seek to become.

To learn more about Dr. Larry Lezotte and Effective Schools Products, visit www.effectiveschools.com or call (517) 349-8841.

Chapter 9

More Effective Schools: Professional Learning Communities in Action

Lawrence W. Lezotte

The Effective Schools movement will celebrate its 40th anniversary in 2006. The history of the Effective Schools movement began with the publication of the Equal Educational Opportunity (EEO) study, also known as the "Coleman Report," in 1966. The now infamous conclusion of that report—that schools do not make a difference—triggered a response that has come to be known as the Effective Schools research. The EEO conclusion was significant because it suggested that if one wanted to know about the achievement of children, one needed to look at the homes from which they came, not the schools in which they learned. Left unchallenged, this conclusion would have essentially rendered schools passive players in helping children achieve the American dream.

In response to this report, a number of independent educational researchers set out to find schools where all children—

especially minority and disadvantaged children—were mastering the intended curriculum. It was thought that finding such schools would serve as compelling evidence that the conclusions of the EEO study were not totally accurate. This successful effort identified many schools that challenged the EEO conclusion that "schools do not make a difference." These initial studies changed the conclusion to "some schools make a difference" and led to the emergence of two new questions:

- Why and how do some schools make a difference?

- Can more schools make a difference?

Why and How Do Some Schools Make a Difference?

The next phase in the evolution of the Effective Schools movement focused on why and how these schools made a difference. The research set out to isolate and describe the critical factors that set the effective schools apart from schools that had similar demographics but were not nearly as effective in terms of measured student achievement. These inquiries identified a series of common characteristics that have come to be known as the Correlates of Effective Schools. The characteristics that were initially described in the early 1970s have remained remarkably stable across many different studies, levels of schooling, and even across countries in diverse areas of the world.

The seven Correlates of Effective Schools are presented in the feature box on the following page. They provide school improvement teams with a comprehensive framework for identifying, categorizing, and solving the problems that schools and school districts face. And because the Correlates are based upon the documented successes of effective schools, they offer hope and inspiration to schools that are struggling to improve. Utilizing the collaborative approach of professional learning communities within this framework will yield a powerful and effective continuous school improvement process leading to increased student achievement for all students.

Can More Schools Make a Difference?

As the correlates began to make their way into various educational publications and were presented at professional conferences, educational leaders from across the nation began to ask the researchers for help in applying the research in their own schools. These requests represented both an opportunity and a challenge. The opportunity was grounded in the shared belief that schools could make a difference if they were guided by the lessons learned from the original studies in the Effective Schools research. The challenge arose from the realization that although the research identified the components of effective schools, it did not clearly identify how these schools had become effective.

The Seven Correlates of Effective Schools

1. Instructional Leadership

2. Clear and Focused Mission

3. Safe and Orderly Environment

4. Climate of High Expectations for Success

5. Frequent Monitoring of Student Progress

6. Positive Home-School Relations

7. Opportunity to Learn and Time on Task

The schools that served as the focus of the Effective Schools research were already effective when they were first identified; now we were being asked to move from describing an existing condition to prescribing how other schools could achieve the same results and become more effective. This would be a challenge, indeed, since we had no idea of the processes the effective schools had used to achieve their unusually high levels of success. Clearly, the schools seeking to emulate their more effective counterparts needed a process and plan of action. Faced with this potential to make a difference in public education and have a positive impact on the achievement of minority and disadvantaged students, we set forth to meet the challenge.

Creating the Effective Schools Process

As we began to think about the challenge, we decided that, as would-be change agents, we would need to practice what we preached. If we were going to ask educators to change their practices based on the Effective Schools research, we would have to use the best available research to guide us in creating a process and a plan of action that had the best possible chance of success. We chose to look at the challenge of school change through three different lenses:

- First, we said that if schools were going to change, then the *people* who work in them would have to change their behaviors to some degree. Therefore, the research that informs this framework would be found by examining characteristics of effective training or staff development programs.

- Second, we said that if schools were going to change, then each *organization* and its operating systems would need to change. This led us to the research on effective organizational and systemic change.

- Finally, we believed that school change, as we conceived it, represented planned or intentional change. With this perspective in mind, we set out to determine what *process* characteristics were associated with effective planned organizational and system change.

Ironically, the characteristics associated with effectiveness of these three different conceptualizations of school change converge, for the most part, around a common list of strategies, including strong and continuing support from leaders and the expertise and time needed for the planning and execution of the change strategies. The first and most compelling success factor was the realization that effective and sustainable change requires commitment from the individuals from whom behavioral change is needed. We concluded that high levels of sustained commitment can only be realized when the affected individuals are involved and engaged in planning the changes they are expected to execute. And the involvement and engagement of others must, in turn, begin with a leader who is personally committed to an inclusive, collaborative process, who is willing to encourage and nurture others to participate and take on leadership roles.

Involvement. The book *Tinkering Toward Utopia* by David Tyack and Larry Cuban (1995) provides a clear and compelling description of why the involvement process is the cornerstone of sustainable school change. The authors note that most efforts to reform schools in the 1900s died on the front steps of the schoolhouse because reforms tended to be launched from outside the school and usually were "top-down." They describe the advocates of these top-down, outside-in reforms as "policy talkers." The teachers and administrators usually had little, if any, voice in shaping the reform efforts. A top-down, outside-in reform effort can be brought to the schoolhouse door without local teacher or administrator involvement. However, we concluded that school reform could be neither successful nor sustainable unless it was embraced by the teachers, administrators, and support staff that define the professional community of that school.

Collaboration. A second book, *The Three Faces of Power*, by internationally recognized economist and scholar Kenneth Boulding (1989), served to buttress the argument for a process that was collaborative in form. Educators often bristle at the notion of using a book about "power" to talk about school reform until they learn more about Boulding's perspective. His work recognized that organizations develop a tremendous inertia to do again what they have always done. The problem of institutional inertia is no less true for schools. Boulding suggests that change advocates must confront institutional inertia by using power to leverage change on the system.

Boulding wrote that there are three forms of power:

1. "Stick power" is the power of threat.

2. "Carrot power" is the power of incentive.

3. "Hug power" is the power derived from shared vision, values, and beliefs.

Boulding concludes that although there are times when you need all three types of power, the greatest of these is "hug power." We found Boulding's observations compelling; they provided us with further support for the collaborative processes that we used to help promote school change based on Effective Schools research.

These sources and others all point to the fact that sustainable change must engage those who are the keepers of the culture in any organization. As a result, our approach to school improvement relies on involvement by a collaborative, school-based school improvement team as the cornerstone and energy source for school-by-school change.

The Core Leadership Group

Our basic approach to establishing and sustaining the collaborative process has involved a small, representative group of the stakeholders in a school: the core leadership group. Generally, we recommend that the team include but not be limited to the principal, a cross section of the teaching faculty, and representatives of noncertified staff members and parents. At the secondary level, we strongly encourage involving students as a part of the core group.

As noted author Peter Block has said, changing an organization begins with changing the *conversation* within the organization (1993). Thus, the leadership team's first responsibility is to initiate and sustain an ongoing conversation of school change based on the Effective Schools research.

The Effective Schools research framework lends itself nicely to engaging a wider circle of staff and other stakeholders. We encourage establishing a cross-sectional team of stakeholders for each of the seven correlates and charging each committee with looking at the school through that lens, finding the relevant research and best practices, and making change recommendations to the core leadership group and the faculty as a whole based on their findings.

The Mission of the Leadership Group

The leadership group has a particular mission and purpose: it is empowered by the school community to serve as trustees of the school's mission. In that regard, they have several duties and responsibilities:

- First, as trustees they are expected to initiate and sustain an ongoing discourse on school improvement.

- Second, they are expected to constantly scan the external educational environment for new research, new ideas, and new possibilities that could improve the school.

- Third, they are expected to constantly examine the internal environment of the school, asking the evaluative question, "Is what we are currently doing working?"

- Fourth, they are expected to monitor the change efforts to ensure they are being implemented and having the desired positive impact on student learning.

- Finally, they are expected to oversee the celebration of successful change efforts.

The Core Beliefs of the Effective Schools Process

Our recommended collaborative process is based on a set of core beliefs that need to be discussed and, once understood, embraced by the school community. The following six beliefs provide further guidance and direction to the collaborative process:

1. School improvement must be school-by-school and one school at a time.

2. There are only two kinds of schools—improving schools and declining schools.

3. Every adult in a school is important.

4. The capacity to improve a school already resides in the school.

5. You and your colleagues are already doing the best you can given what you know and the current conditions in which you find yourself.

6. All children can learn and the school controls enough of the variables to assure that virtually all students do learn.

1. School improvement must be school-by-school and one school at a time. We have had our best success when the collaborative processes are in place within school-wide groups. In our experience, collaborative groups that bring together stakeholders from several schools at the same time do not work well. For example, some districts have created district-wide elementary reading teams. While there is a place for such conversations, they do not substitute for the conversations of a school-level team.

Likewise, we have not seen great success with collaborative groups that represent only a small segment of the school. For example, grade-level groups have a place in school change, but we have had more success with teams that represent the school as a whole and focus on a particular topic or area of organizational interest, such as a school that chooses to incorporate a focus on literacy across all content areas. The need for school-wide conversation is especially important when schools are struggling to create the vertical and horizontal curriculum alignment demanded by the standards and accountability movement today. However, despite the lack of success we have seen with these two strategies, we believe that school reforms must always be adapted to fit the context of the individual school if they are to be successful and sustained.

2. There are only two kinds of schools—improving schools and declining schools. This core belief directly confronts an unspoken assumption held by some educators: the assumption of "the status quo school." The standards and accountability movement, No Child Left Behind (NCLB), and other governmental reform policies define the reality of schools today. Taken together, they virtually eliminate the status quo option. According to author Jack Bowsher (2001) in his book *Fix Schools First,* even the highest achieving schools in the United States have upwards of 30% of their students failing to meet the grade-level standards of NCLB. Within this context, a status quo school would be described as a declining school, and educators clinging to this concept of the status quo school as "average" would be misguided.

Obviously, most educators would rather be associated with improvement than decline. When a school embraces this belief, the conversation moves from "Should we seek reform?" to "What reforms should we pursue?" Since schools are not only expected to improve, but also to improve quickly, this shift in the conversation is significant in providing the impetus for immediate action.

3. Every adult in a school is important. A strong argument can be made that no one is more important in achieving the learning mission of a school than the teacher. On the other hand, a school's culture is maintained through the actions of virtually every adult in every role in the school. As a result, the quality of life in a school community is enhanced when all the members of that community understand and accept their roles, rights, and responsibilities. For example, high school guidance counselors play a critical role in communicating high or low expectations to students. Therefore, if reform is to be effectively and efficiently implemented, the change process must reach out and give voice to all the keepers of the culture to secure their commitment.

4. The capacity to improve a school already resides in the school. Often schools come to believe that the resources needed to change a school reside outside the school. This belief, when unchallenged, seems to provide a level of comfort to those who hold this view by placing the responsibility for change beyond their control. Certainly external resources of one sort or another can often facilitate the reform effort. Nonetheless, there is virtually no limit to what schools can do to improve, despite an initial lack of resources, if the stakeholders join together in a common commitment to change. It has been said that we find the time and resources to do those things that we value. When stakeholders highly value a common vision of "learning for all," they become very creative in finding the necessary time and resources for making the vision a reality. My colleague Ron Edmonds best conveyed this sentiment when addressing a school faculty. He would remind them that they already knew more than they needed to know to improve the school. He would go on to say that whether or not they did so would ultimately come down to how they felt about the fact that they had not done it so far.

5. You and your colleagues are already doing the best you can given what you know and the current conditions in which you find yourself. A major source of resistance once the collaborative conversation begins comes from individuals who believe that a call for change implies that they are negligent and not doing a good job. This core belief addresses this concern by acknowledging that professionals are already doing the best they can given what they know. If that is accepted as true, we know that successful sustainable change will require that new knowledge make its way into the school and to its staff. The collaborative team process provides an ideal vehicle for continuous professional learning.

Sustainable change in a school requires not only change in the knowledge of the staff, but also in the conditions that make up the school as a network of interdependent components. Usually, the successful implementation of new knowledge requires change in one or more of the components in the system. This could mean a change in the instructional delivery system, scheduling, student grouping, staff development, or any other component of the school's structural, personnel, or instructional systems.

6. All children can learn and the school controls enough of the variables to assure that virtually all students do learn. This is the most important belief that provides the foundation for school improvement based on the Effective Schools research. Before we address the challenges to this belief, we need to be clear. This belief does not say that all children can learn the same day, at the same rate, or in the same way. As a matter of fact, one of the keys to successful "learning for all" is based on the willingness of the school staff to customize and differentiate its services to meet the specific needs of each student.

Once the empowered school community embraces this belief and begins to open up to the possibility of "learning for all," the question then becomes, "What needs to change to make this possible?" Our experience verifies that the possibilities are unlimited once a dedicated school staff goes in search of research and best practices to advance their shared vision of learning for all. However, until they embrace the possibility that all children can learn, the obstacles and barriers they will find are virtually endless and will seem insurmountable.

Professional Learning Communities in Action

School improvement efforts based on the Effective Schools framework have grown steadily since the 1970s. The number of individual schools and school districts that have used this process as their strategy has been difficult to calculate because no one agency or individual is responsible for keeping such information. We do know, however, that whole states, such as Texas, have used the Effective Schools framework as the required process for campus accreditation. We know that many of the regional accreditation agencies have modified their processes and now expect schools to use this basic framework as part of their accreditation efforts. We know that reforms in Federal Title I policies direct schools toward this framework for school-wide improvement planning. Finally, we know that the core ideas of No Child Left Behind—such as the required disaggregation of assessment scores—were directly influenced by the Effective Schools research and improvement framework. The evolution of the Effective Schools movement and its success over time provides evidence of the necessity and sustainability of professional learning communities.

Continuous school improvement based on the Effective Schools research has a long and proud history of improving student achievement when the processes of change are implemented with fidelity and sustained over time. We have found that when schools adopt the Effective Schools research as a common language, incorporate the research on effective teaching practices, and then take steps to assure that all staff members are grounded in these concepts, the essential ingredients for improvement are at hand. When we empower an ever-enlarging conversation of school change by engaging a leadership team and other study groups, the essential processes for continuous learning and change begin to stir. Finally, when the system provides the time for teams to meet and learn how to learn together, the momentum for sustainable change steadily builds.

The concept of the professional learning community was not part of the school improvement lexicon when the Effective Schools journey began. It would have been easier and more efficient to engage schools in the conversations around the research if it had been. Nonetheless, without taking unreasonable revisionist liberties when we look back over the last 40 years of efforts to improve schools based on Effective Schools research, it seems fair to say that the philosophy and core concepts of professional learning communities have been essential components of the process. Clearly, continuous school improvement based on the Effective Schools research is an example of professional learning communities in action.

References

Block, J. H., Everson, S. T., & Guskey, T. R. (Eds.). (1995). *School improvement programs.* New York: Scholastic Inc.

Block, P. (1987). *The empowered manager: Positive political skills at work.* San Francisco: Jossey-Bass.

Block, P. (1993). *Stewardship: Choosing service over self-interest.* San Francisco: Berrett-Koehler.

Boulding, K. E. (1989). *The three faces of power*. Newbury Park, CA: SAGE Publications.

Bowsher, J. E. (2001). *Fix schools first*. Gaithersburg, MD: Aspen Publishers.

Coleman, J. S., Campbell, E. Q., Hobson, C. J., McPartland, J., Mood, A. M., Weinfeld, F. D., & York, R. L. (1966). *Equality of educational opportunity*. Washington, DC: National Center for Educational Statistics, Department of Health, Education, and Welfare.

Lezotte, L. W. (1997). *Learning for all*. Okemos, MI: Effective Schools Products, Ltd.

Lezotte, L. W., & McKee, K. M. (2002). *Assembly required: A continuous school improvement system*. Okemos, MI: Effective Schools Products, Ltd.

Tyack, D., & Cuban, L. (1995). *Tinkering toward utopia: A century of public school reform*. Cambridge, MA: Harvard University Press.

Barbara Eason-Watkins

No school leader has risen through the ranks of the Chicago Public Schools (CPS) faster than Dr. Barbara Eason-Watkins, who went directly from the principalship to the second-ranking position in the district—chief education officer. As principal, she won national recognition for developing McCosh Elementary School into a model professional learning community. As chief education officer, she is leading the effort to replicate that success across the entire district. As Richard Elmore of Harvard University observed, "The thing that's important to understand about what she's doing and about what's going on in Chicago is nobody's tried to do this work on this scale." The *Chicago Sun Times* recently named her as one of the most powerful women in Chicago.

In this chapter, Dr. Eason-Watkins describes the challenges of developing the capacity of staff to build professional learning communities across an urban district that includes over 620 schools, 45,000 employees, and 434,000 students. The challenge was made even more formidable by legislation that gave considerable control of individual schools to elected bodies of parents, teachers, and community representatives. How could a district office launch and lead improvement initiatives in a system designed to provide authority and control to individual schools and their local communities?

Dr. Eason-Watkins describes how CPS attempted to build shared vision throughout the district by building shared knowledge and clarifying the goals and priorities of the system. She explains the structural changes that were initiated to support schools in their efforts to adopt PLC practices. She outlines the district's attempt to balance systems of accountability that convey a clear expectation of improvement with essential support for staff. She recognizes that the ultimate success of the initiative depends on changing not only the structure, but also the culture of the entire system.

For additional information about Dr. Barbara Eason-Watkins, visit www.cps.k12.il.us/AboutCPS/people/Eason-Watkins/eason-watkins.html.

Chapter 10

Implementing PLCs in the Chicago Public Schools

Barbara Eason-Watkins

Now more than ever before, principals and instructional leaders are acknowledging that a critical element to raising student achievement and sustaining successful schools is a strong professional learning community that is inclusive of all teachers, educators, and principals. On a local school level, a proactive principal with a hands-on approach can foster and nurture such a culture that supports and validates a shared and articulated mission, vision, and core values and is focused on continuous improvement and action. How can a similar culture or model of shared leadership and vision be replicated on a district level? Is it possible for a school system to create and sustain policies, procedures, and structures that encourage, support, and reinforce professional learning communities within and across all schools? Beginning in 2001, the Chicago Public Schools embarked on an ambitious and dynamic path to do just that.

Chicago Public Schools currently has over 620 schools, 45,000 employees, and 434,000 students with 84.9% of students coming from low-income families and 14.5% having only limited English proficiency. The 1988 School Reform Act gave local control of schools to Local School Councils (LSCs)—elected bodies made up of parent, community, and teacher representatives. In 1995, the mayor of the city of Chicago, Richard M. Daley, was given control of the school system, bringing a new level of accountability, administrative services, and clear performance measures to all schools.

When I first became chief education officer for the Chicago Public Schools in 2001, our teachers, principals, and system-wide educators were distracted and overwhelmed by daily administrative, clerical, organizational, security, and maintenance demands—much like many large urban school districts. Learning was secondary for principals who were consumed by the daily trials and tribulations of managing a school. While some of our schools, several in disadvantaged neighborhoods, were able to build effective communities where adults were successfully engaging students in learning, these examples were rare and often sustainable only by an individual dynamic leader or specific funding source. To take the Chicago Public Schools to the next level where every child in every school is provided a quality education, it was necessary to transform the ethos of the system. As a district, like in an individual school, we had to organizationally support learning communities and validate collaboration, innovation, and accountability.

Three significant steps were required to create real change and alter a culture built upon the notion of local control (the 1988 School Reform Act) and individualism among schools:

- The first step was to develop, establish, and articulate a clear and common vision and mission for the Chicago Public Schools.

- The second step was to organizationally support this vision by realigning resources and creating incentives and opportunities for change.

- Finally, we had to commit to allowing the time for real change and growth to occur.

Steps Toward a Shared Vision: The Education Plan

Initially, when the new administration began the planning process, we knew that a key element had to be to design a process or structure that enabled principals and leadership teams to:

- Frequently interact and plan quality instruction

- Draw on one another's expertise

- Look at students' work

- Build common practices

We also acknowledged that the role of developing, facilitating, and sustaining this process could no longer be the sole responsibility of the school or an individual. Instead, to create real change, it was vital that the central office reach out to the people and structures we were looking to change. Transforming communities and professional environments could not be a top-down command; instead, it had to be embraced and accepted by the entire system.

In 2001, the Chicago Public Schools (CPS) underwent an intensive assessment, planning, and program development process with the intent of producing a clear vision for the district. CPS identified overarching themes and challenges throughout the system with the assistance of hundreds of administrators, principals, teachers, staff, parents, students, community members, and partners. Using focus groups as the vehicle to extract new ideas and diagnose systematic challenges, CPS drew upon the expertise from those who successfully, and not so successfully, were functioning within and outside the system on a daily basis. Time, resources, support, and coherence were some of the major obstacles preventing meaningful change and ongoing collaboration on a local level—all similar to the challenges faced in other public school districts. Simply stated, learning communities were not a district priority and the leadership was not always in place for schools to develop their own.

Over a year of research and planning efforts culminated with the release of *The Education Plan for the Chicago Public Schools* in 2002. The Education Plan presented all schools, staff, parents, and stakeholders with a clear purpose and eight specific goals for the district—goals that could only be achieved by a transformation that developed new capacity at the classroom, school, and district levels.

The district's commitment to use professional learning concepts as the foundation for its improvement initiative was made evident by the first three goals of the Education Plan. Those goals stated:

1. Build instructional capacity that provides students with differentiated, engaging, and challenging curriculum and strong instructional programs for all grade levels.

2. Develop innovative and rigorous approaches to recruiting, developing, supporting, and retaining high-quality teaching and leadership.

3. Maintain schools with strong communities of learning where teams of teachers work with the principal and other school staff to create a work and school environment of problem solving, innovation, reflection on practice, and collaborative professional development to design and implement effective instructional programs.

One of the major achievements of the Education Plan was its success in establishing the shared vision, language, and goals of the district. By openly communicating frameworks and strategies to overcome the challenges articulated in the plan, change, although presumably difficult, was understood and welcomed on many levels.

Two of the major challenges recognized early on and throughout the plan were organization and capacity. Structurally, CPS was not organized to relieve principals and school leaders from their daily managerial tasks. Even when time permitted some attention to instruction and professional development, there was a significant disparity among the capacities of our instructional leaders. Many principals were not equipped with or even able to access the resources and supports to take their schools to the next level. To address these needs, CPS reorganized into a more supportive and instructionally focused "area structure" and began recruiting teams of educators from schools to participate in School Teams Achieving Results for Students (STARS), which I will explain in detail later in this chapter.

CPS Area Instruction Offices:
Laying a Strong Foundation for PLCs in Every School

In 2002, the Education Plan reorganized the district from six regional offices into 24 instructional areas to ensure proactive support to schools for increasing instructional capacity and improving student achievement. Therefore, instead of having 60 to 80 schools to monitor and assist, each area now had 20 to 40. An area is led by an area instruction officer (AIO) who is in charge of two area teams: one focuses on instructional support and one focuses on management support. The instructional support team is made up of highly qualified content specialists who meet regularly with CPS curriculum offices to identify system-wide and area-specific priorities and who work as a team to provide targeted professional development and support in their area's schools.

The area structure has had both the intended and unintended benefits of building instructional and leadership capacity, providing coherence across the district, bringing the school-based implementation perspective to the development of central office policies and initiatives, creating a system-wide focus on student learning, and instituting data-driven decision-making.

Building instructional and leadership capacity. The reorganization into instructional areas furthered district efforts by promoting the establishment of structures that focus on student learning. Shared study and reflection on professional practice for all AIOs and principals have become significant components of establishing learning communities at the district level and for principals within each of the areas. The AIOs meet on a regular basis to examine and reflect on their professional practice by reading professional books and discussing current research in teaching, learning, and educational leadership. The monthly professional development for principals concentrates on increasing the instructional leadership capacity. The focus of what it means to be a principal in the Chicago Public Schools is now on instructional leadership and facilitating the change process—rather than on site management.

Area instruction officers also lead area team learning communities that reflect on their professional practice and determine strategies for working in schools. Each team is responsible for building the capacity of school teams to improve student achievement. The importance of building a professional learning community is evident in how the Education Plan outlines the instructional support each area team must provide:

- Instructional coaching and mentoring

- Support for building professional learning communities at the school level

- Study groups for common problems and common professional development activities

- Formative and summative data for continuous monitoring of instruction

The learning community, therefore, is modeled and developed at the district level with the AIOs, at the area level with area teams, among the area principals at monthly professional development activities, and by the area instruction team in the work they do with the schools.

The school walk-through: A system-wide focus on student learning. Another critical district structure for improving student learning and the development of learning communities is the school walk-through. Area teams participate in instructional walk-throughs with school leadership teams. The central focus of all school walk-throughs is how student achievement can be improved. Specifically, the driving questions are:

1. Are the students learning?

2. How do we know?

3. How does this inform our professional development needs for addressing the gaps?

School walk-throughs support and promote the development of a learning community in a number of ways. Initially, school teams, which include both building administrators and teachers, participated with the area team in looking for evidence that addresses one of the questions listed above. The following focus questions are frequently used by CPS during walk-throughs:

- Are the objectives of the lesson clearly understood by students and aligned with learning activities?

- Are the students actively engaged in the lesson?

- Are the students receiving explicit instruction and scaffolding prior to independent work?

- Does the classroom environment support and stimulate student learning?

- Is the teacher lecturing or facilitating learning?

During the walk-through, classroom experiences are viewed through the eyes of the learner, adding to the emphasis on student-centeredness. Teams discuss and reflect on the evidence collected, and results-oriented short- and long-term action plans are developed for subsequent discussion by the faculty. Action plans generally address the professional development needed to make the identified improvements. In the third year of the area restructuring, the primary responsibility for conducting regular walk-throughs was delegated to the principals and their school teams.

Data-driven decision-making. The emphasis on assessments and evaluations that drive instructional practices has led CPS to embrace the use of data analysis to shape decisions on a district, area, school, and even classroom level. To allow for data to be accessible to all stakeholders, the district has utilized the *Grow Network* (www.grownetwork.com), a system of integrated print reports, web tools, instructional materials, and professional development opportunities that transforms the results of large-scale assessments into clear and effective tools for action. The *Grow Network* provides easier accessibility to aggregated and disaggregated data. Area offices provide professional development for principals in effective use of the *Grow Network* and area instructional technology coaches support this training.

Additionally, CPS is in the process of developing and implementing an Instructional Management Program and Academic Communication Tool (IMPACT). IMPACT is a far-reaching technology solution designed to provide a strong foundation for data-driven decision making and to offer technological support to the district's educational and administrative priorities. Through Schoolnet, an instruction management component of IMPACT, teachers will be able to map out their students' assessment results against state and national standards and their curriculum, enabling them to modify instruction immediately. Once fully implemented, the IMPACT solution will replace out-of-date and inefficient systems and information networks and be used throughout the district by administrators, teachers, support staff, central office staff, and parents.

CPS has also made significant efforts in overcoming barriers related to time. By extending the school day, the district banks time for regular professional development at the school, area, and district levels. Leadership capacity and shared responsibility are enhanced when teachers use restructured time for selecting, planning, and delivering the necessary professional development for improvements that lead to increased student learning.

The school perspective on district-wide decision-making. Area instructional officers also serve as vital voices in central office decision-making. As CPS creates, revises, and replaces rules, policies, and initiatives that impact schools, it has become customary to consult AIOs. As senior staff members who directly oversee principals, the AIOs' perspectives, expertise, and experiences have helped a system with over 600 principals to work more effectively on a daily basis at the school level.

The district has moved forward in its efforts to build and sustain a professional learning community that has every child at its center by the restructuring of the district into area instruction offices, the placement of successful and effective school leaders as AIOs, the focus on student learning via school walk-throughs, the modeling of study and reflection on practice at the district and area levels, the creation of collaborative structures for school improvement (such as restructured days), and the district-wide emphasis on results orientation.

School Teams Achieving Results for Students (STARS)

While reorganizing the system into instructional areas has created a foundation for professional learning communities, direct support to schools is necessary to invoke real and sustainable change. The School Teams Achieving Results for Students (STARS) program was one of the initiatives developed by the CPS Office of Professional Development to help CPS provide that ongoing support.

Program design. STARS is a comprehensive research-based professional development program that focuses on improving both instruction and student achievement through school-based leadership teams. Mid-tier schools were invited to participate in this district-funded professional development program. One hundred thirty-five school-based teams (each consisting of a principal and four teacher leaders) were selected to participate in year one of STARS.

STARS was developed as a multi-year program in order to introduce, reinforce, and support the strategies and skills being presented and cultivated by the training. In year one, school teams participated in a 5-day summer institute (35 hours), six follow-up sessions, ongoing coaching, and a culminating learning fair to share school implementation and progress. During the summer institute and follow-up sessions, teams participated in professional development that focused on implementing differentiated instruction, higher-order thinking skills, using data for decision-making, and looking at student work. During year two, continuing school teams reviewed previous learning, reinforced and extended building professional learning community skills for the purpose of school-based problem-solving, and gleaned new research-based instructional strategies and information.

This sustained approach to professional development over time provided school-based teams with the opportunity to obtain new knowledge, to go back to their schools to apply it, and to return to their broader, system-level professional learning community to share and gather new ideas, strategies, and feedback. This format proved to be invaluable to the teams as they challenged their fears and developed increased confidence about going back to their schools in their new roles as teacher leaders in instruction and professional development.

The program design focused on improving instruction and student achievement by combining the knowledge of change with instructional leadership and a focus on improving learning. The instructional component is based on the proven best practices as documented by Marzano, Pickering, and Pollock in *Classroom Instruction That Works* (2001). The program builds on the research that shows that teacher leadership and ongoing learning are positively correlated with increased student achievement (Newmann, 2000). Training has been provided by a team of consultants from the Ontario Institute for Studies in Education at the University of Toronto. These consultants possess diverse experiences in leading large-scale change projects across North America. They have provided assistance to the system for the past 6 years in a range of instructional and leadership training projects that have helped build capacity systematically. The district provided local coaching support for schools. By combining current research with application to school issues, teachers and principals were engaged in cooperative learning groups, viewed videos, took part in simulations, and participated in both small- and large-group discussions. The program modules consisted of six components:

1. Building School Capacity

2. Understanding and Managing Change

3. Designing Powerful Teaching and Learning

4. Building Professional Learning Communities

5. Developing the School Leadership Team

6. Planning for Action

Impact. Although no quantitative data are available at this time, the first phase of program implementation has resulted in expanded instructional capacity for many schools with instruction that is differentiated, engaging, challenging, and based on proven best practices. With time and experience, schools have reported high success rates in implementing new STARS strategies with and among teachers across grade levels and content areas—especially in literacy. Teachers have shared that they appreciated being able to break the isolation of working alone to learn from other colleagues and being able to share, reflect, and analyze their practices as part of a collective learning community.

As a result of their professional development in STARS, teachers have had the opportunity to hone their leadership skills and to work in conjunction with the principal to plan, design, and facilitate professional development for the school staff during teacher institute days and restructured days. Principals have shared that they have gained knowledge, skills, and confidence in being more effective professional developers and instructional leaders. They have also reported gaining knowledge and experience in sharing leadership with teachers.

Principals and teachers gained skills in applying a broad range of research-based instructional strategies and information. They learned strategies to facilitate and influence individual and organizational change, and they gained knowledge in current research to build school capacity for increased student achievement. They obtained experience in building professional learning communities and in designing ongoing school-based professional development. Training sessions have provided a venue for sharing challenges and ideas with other school-based teams, thus helping to build upon school and system capacity.

In years one and two of STARS, the district was able to provide the funding necessary to implement the model. Funding was limited for the third year (2004-2005) for continuing schools or for schools new to the STARS program. Therefore, schools wishing to participate in STARS were required to pay for the program from local discretionary funds. At this time there are 13 returning schools and 3 new schools. There is a strong possibility that grant funding will become available for at least 50 new schools and 50 returning schools.

STARS has proven to be an effective model to help build instructional capacity, to transform school culture, and to help build professional learning communities, but cuts in funding have impeded broader school- and system-level participation. As with most programs and initiatives, sustainability, commitment, leadership, and funding are critical to its success.

The Future of Professional Learning Communities in Chicago

Chicago Public Schools has made it a priority to develop and support initiatives and programs that help it reach the vision outlined in our Education Plan. With the area structures, we now have a system that focuses on instructional leadership, best practices, and capacity building. With targeted programs like STARS, we can provide the resources and models for schools to foster and embrace local collaboration, team-building, and shared responsibilities. As CPS continues to transform its culture, it is vital that we also alter and raise the expectations of our leaders and staff.

Being a principal in the Chicago Public Schools now means being willing and able to establish and sustain a professional learning community in a school. A change in perspective is required so that shared leadership is not viewed as a matter of style, but as a value the system holds. As we allocate resources to increase the capacity of current principals and educators, CPS is recruiting aspiring principals and teachers who will promote a culture that values and builds professional learning communities.

Finally, CPS is transforming the model by which the system provides services and makes decisions. Areas and principals are being empowered with the resources to decide what works best for their school communities. One size does not fit all, and in order to respect the work and priorities of local teams, CPS is building flexibility and transparency into its procedures and programs.

The district continues to face challenges for putting structures in place that will ensure a fundamental shift in thinking. There will always be bureaucratic and resource constraints. But as the system continues to prioritize and respect school- and area-based professional learning communities, we can support the practice of student-centered learning as a district.

References

Marzano, R. J., Pickering, D. J., & Pollock, J. E. (2001). *Classroom instruction that works: Research-based strategies for increasing student achievement.* Alexandria, VA: Association for Supervision and Curriculum Development.

Newmann, F. M. (2000). *Professional development to build organizational capacity in low-achieving schools: Promising strategies and future challenges.* Madison, WI: Wisconsin Center for Education Research.

Michael Fullan

Dr. Michael Fullan, former dean of the Ontario Institute for Studies in Education of the University of Toronto, is widely recognized as an international authority on educational reform. His ideas on leadership, the change process, and school improvement are studied throughout the world. Some of his more acclaimed books include the series *What's Worth Fighting For* (with Andy Hargeaves); *Change Forces; The New Meaning of Educational Change; The Moral Imperative of School Leadership; and Leadership and Sustainability: System Thinkers in Action.*

Dr. Fullan is active in training, consulting, and evaluating change projects throughout the world, and he recently led the evaluation team that conducted the assessment of England's National Literacy and Numeracy Strategy. He is special advisor to the Premier and Minister of Education in Ontario.

In this chapter, Dr. Fullan acknowledges that there is an increasingly clear picture of the nature and importance of schools that function as professional learning communities, but he contends such schools will remain rare and transitory if the larger system of education is not examined and improved. He offers the concept of "tri-level development" as the best strategy to increase the capacity of the larger system to build and sustain professional learning communities. This solution focuses on what needs to be done at three levels of the larger educational system: the school/community level, the district or regional level, and the state or provincial policy level.

Dr. Fullan regards the ability of leaders to develop other leaders as key to the success of the tri-level strategy. He cautions, however, that individual educators should not assume his call for systems change and enlightened leadership absolves them from personal responsibility for doing what they can to bring about meaningful change in their own setting. As he concludes, "professional learning communities writ large is everyone's agenda across the tri-levels."

For more information about Dr. Michael Fullan and his work, go to www.michaelfullan.com.

Chapter 11

Professional Learning Communities Writ Large

Michael Fullan

We have an increasingly clear picture of the nature and importance of professional learning communities in schools. We now understand that such communities do not merely represent congeniality. Rather, they dig deeply into learning. They engage in disciplined inquiry and continuous improvement in order to "raise the bar" and "close the gap" of student learning and achievement.

We have seen in the work of Newmann, King, and Youngs (2000) that effective schools develop the collective capacity of the full staff to improve achievement through:

- Developing teachers' skills
- Improving the quality of ongoing interaction among staff
- Achieving a coherent focus
- Mobilizing resources
- Developing school leadership

DuFour (2004, reprinted on page 31) and the other authors in this book describe professional learning communities as contributing to high performance by:

- Ensuring that all students learn

- Fostering a culture of collaboration

- Focusing on results

We do, in other words, know a great deal about professional learning communities at the school level. In this chapter, I seek to place professional learning communities in a larger perspective. I will argue that if we do not examine and improve the overall system at three levels, we will never have more than temporary havens of excellence that come and go. Without attention to the larger system, professional learning communities will always be in the minority, never rising above 20% in popularity in the nation, and will not last beyond the tenure of those fortunate enough to have established temporary collaborative cultures.

The Tri-Level Solution

In my most recent work, I am pursuing through specific initiatives what I call the "tri-level solution." The tri-level solution involves three levels:

- The school/community level

- The district or regional level

- The state or province policy level

This solution represents a total system focus—a self-conscious attempt at all levels to use best knowledge to strategize and bring about improvements and build capacity. Capacity-building is the development and use of policies, strategies, and actions that increase the collective power or efficacy of whole groups, organizations, or systems to engage in continuous improvement for ongoing student learning. Typically, capacity-building synergizes three powerful collective phenomena:

- New skills and dispositions
- More focused and enhanced resources
- Greater shared commitment, cohesion, and motivation

In professional learning communities writ large, the system as a whole adopts the agenda of fostering deep learning communities. In other words, schools and communities explicitly pursue the development of new cultures of professional learning; districts, regions, and schools establish infrastructures to support and monitor such development; and states or provinces commit themselves to policies and strategies for systemically addressing the evolution of professional learning cultures. This is a tri-level solution because it builds capacity across the three levels.

The school/community level. We know a fair amount about professional learning communities at the school/community level, although our knowledge of how parents and communities contribute to student learning is much less developed. What Newmann, King, and Youngs (2000) found is particularly instructive. They examined individual schools that had the high collective capacity to bring about improved student achievement. They then asked the question, "Where does this capacity come from?" They suggested that, in theory, individual school capacity could come from policies and programs at the district and state level. As they examined this potential link, they could find no evidence that school capacity to bring about improved achievement was caused by the external infrastructure working to produce it. If the infrastructure did not help develop school capacity, then what did?

My own view is that it was largely a matter of luck or serendipity that these schools developed a high capacity. The right principal came along, certain teachers gravitated to this principal, the chemistry was great, and the group experienced cohesion and success. When this happens, it is wonderful—as long as it lasts. So if the infrastructure is not systematically working on capacity-building in the school, professional learning communities will occur in only a minority number of cases and will not last beyond the tenure of the right leader or group.

The district or regional level. Because of the limitations of working on individual school-based professional learning communities, we and others began to work with whole districts with the goal of building capacity with all or the vast majority of schools in a district. In the same way that professional learning communities refer to the *culture of the school*, we have shifted our perspective to the *culture of the district*. The question then becomes, "How do entire districts become professional learning communities where all groups (within and across schools) exemplify professional learning communities in action?"

We have worked with over a dozen districts in Canada, the United States, England, and Australia to help build district-wide capacity in order to raise the bar and close the gap of student achievement at the district level. Reports on district-wide success experienced by others are now appearing in the literature. Fullan, Bertani, and Quinn (2004) found that districts successful in their capacity-building had the following characteristics:

1. Leaders with a coherent driving conceptualization

2. A collective moral purpose

3. The structure and roles most effective for developing capacity-building

4. Leadership and capacity-building for those in key roles

5. Lateral capacity building

6. Deep learning

7. Productive conflict

8. Demanding cultures

9. External partners

10. Growing financial investment

When district leadership understands the change process and the corresponding capacity-building, they appreciate what needs to be done. They in turn foster a collective moral purpose, organize the structure and roles most effectively, provide ongoing leadership development for those in key roles, and formulate strategies where schools learn from each other (lateral capacity-building). They pursue deeper learning agendas, appreciate that conflict is part and parcel of moving forward, raise expectations of all to achieve more, and seek external partners and resources that enable them to go even further.

This success has been largely confined to elementary and middle schools. There are no examples, as far as I know, of district-wide high school reform where all or most of the high schools in the district have established professional learning communities collectively as a district. This is partly because high school reform is more complex and more difficult, and partly because we have not tried until recently. There are now several ongoing major reform initiatives in the four countries mentioned previously, so we should expect to see in the near future examples of high school reform across whole districts.

When district leaders understand and use the knowledge base represented by these 10 components, they will see district-wide success. It is critical, then, that the first two levels—school/community and district/regional—depend upon and reinforce the work of one another.

The next logical question is this: "Where does district-level capacity come from?" One could speculate that state or federal level policies and programs help foster district-level capacity across the whole state or country. Alas, this is not the case. District-wide reform remains in the minority and, like individual school success, it probably does not last beyond the tenure of one or two superintendents and school boards.

The state or province level. This takes us to the third level in the tri-level solution: state or province policy. This policy level is the most difficult to develop because of its political complexity and its propensity to favor quick and inevitably superficial solutions. There is a natural political tendency to focus on accountability because it is easy to legislate change in this area. Capacity-building, on the other hand, is more difficult and requires time and cultivation. Accountability without capacity-building amounts to little or no gain.

What we need instead is for those at the third level—the state policy makers—to become knowledgeable and action-oriented about fostering capacity-building along with accountability. I cannot emphasize enough that this involves learning how to think and act accordingly. Policy makers must become deliberate learners in the same way that an effective principal is a self-reflective learner and a successful superintendent conceptualizes and solves problems.

Becoming more knowledgeable requires that policy makers become increasingly familiar with the value and concepts of professional knowledge communities. It requires that they begin to think and act differently by appointing new leaders to the central team, to pass different policies, and to formulate different strategies that integrate accountability and capacity-building with a focus on results. They must also refocus and enhance the investment of resources to support capacity-building as a fundamental characteristic of the system.

There are a small and growing number of examples of system-level engagement in capacity-building. England was the first to do so. In 1997 when the Blair government was first elected, it designed an integrated strategy that combined "pressure and support" to focus on literacy and numeracy. There was a strong accountability emphasis, but at the same time there was a major orchestrated strategy to increase the capacity of teachers and school principals to work together to achieve new levels of student achievement. The outcome was impressive with large gains achieved. Sixty-two percent of 11-year-olds were at proficiency levels in 1997 in literacy; for numeracy, the figure was 61%. By 2002, the scores had reached 75% for literacy and 73% for numeracy. This represents a remarkable accomplishment because the whole system—some 20,000 schools—moved forward. All this was achieved within one election period—less than 4 years. It did, however, raise some difficult questions concerning sustained reform.

The gains in literacy and numeracy leveled off, or plateaued, by 2001. The scores in 2001, 2002, and 2003 were identical. The initial highly centrally driven, very supportive strategy was effective—but only to a point. To go beyond the plateau requires a deeper strategy of addressing the "hearts and minds" of teachers and principals. This is not a straightforward issue because the additional gains must be real and achieved on a large scale in the system as a whole (Fullan, 2005b).

The plateau problem notwithstanding, large systems are now engaging in accomplishing large-scale reform. As we have seen, England has had significant success. More recently, the province of Ontario, South Australia, and Washington state are all explicitly focusing on tri-level reform strategies in which the goal is to develop each level and their interrelationships.

State-Level Development

In the cases of state-level development that we have studied, state policy makers began to gain new knowledge (they began to take seriously the growing knowledge base on capacity building, professional learning communities, and the like); they began to think differently; and they began to act differently as reflected in the policies they promoted, the strategies they formulated, the leaders they appointed, and the resources they allocated (they both refocused and enhanced financial investments fuelled by their growing success).

In all of these cases, entire systems are actively engaged in tri-level reform, where the criterion of success is large-scale development of all three levels, and the outcome is an increase in collective capacity for continuous improvement and greater accomplishments in "raising the bar" and "closing the gap" in student performance.

Tri-level development promotes professional learning communities as a *system* quality. We are by no means there yet, but the cases we have observed are extremely promising. For the first time, we are seeing improvement on a very large scale, not just in isolated schools.

Four Implications

There are four implications to the tri-level solution I describe:

1. The need to address the problem of bias toward individualistic solutions.

2. The radical need for systems thinkers in action.

3. The importance of learning from each other as we go.

4. The danger of waiting for others to act.

Bias toward individualistic solutions. The bias toward individuals concerns policies and strategies that look like they are intended to change the system, but upon closer inspection, it is clear that they change individuals and not the system. I am referring to state policies that provide new standards for teacher education, for professional learning, for educational leaders, and so on. These are crucial, but by themselves they represent only about thirty percent of the solution. They are necessary but not sufficient for system-wide change.

Let us take the professional learning component of standards as a case in point. All of the new standards for teacher education, leadership, and professional learning contain components that emphasize collaboration with and learning from others. The assumption is that if we produce enough individuals with these new characteristics, they will change the system.

The truth is that the system changes individuals more often than individuals change the system. In addition to the appropriate standards, we need to focus directly on changing cultures so that there is a growing opportunity to *learn in context.*

In fact, the tri-level solution examples in the previous section all involved altering cultures (at the school, district, and state levels) so that people *experience* the new values and behaviors in their day-to-day actions. When people learn new things in context, two powerful things happen:

1. The new learning is specific to the context in which they are working.

2. Because the learning occurs in context, people are learning with others so that the outcome is shared learning and further changes in the culture.

Radical need for system thinkers in action. "System thinking in action" (Fullan, 2005a) addresses sustainability and the need to change context. Professional learning communities writ large means *changing cultures to create new contexts.* How do contexts or systems change? They do so over a very long period of time. System change evolves as a result of major alterations in demographics, technology, and other social forces. But we want to accelerate the development of good changes like the spread of professional learning communities. The key to this involves conceptualizing sustainability and using leadership to change context or the environment by (1) increasing leaders' participation in wider contexts and (2) helping to develop leadership in others so they can do the same.

After about 2 years of working on district-wide reform, my colleagues and I noticed the following phenomenon: Individual school principals became almost as concerned about the success of other schools in the district as they were with the success of their own school. This is a direct result of being engaged in a larger purpose and getting to know other schools through walk-throughs and other lateral capacity-building strategies. These strategies might involve small clusters of schools working together to improve literacy or principals and teachers conducting walk-throughs of a school or schools to provide critical feedback to the staff. Their world-views and commitments increased to encompass the larger system, but at the same time, they helped change the very system within which they work. They literally changed their context.

The key to sustainability is to change context. Hargreaves and Fink (in press) put it this way: "Sustainability does not simply mean whether something will last. It addresses how particular initiatives can be developed without compromising the development of others in the surrounding environment now and in the future." Sustainability is about changing and developing the social environment. Professional learning communities writ large is not about the proliferation of single schools; it is about creating new environments across the system through tri-level development.

The following eight items (Fullan, 2005a) are elements of sustainability and part of the writ large agenda:

1. Public service with a moral purpose is an explicit commitment on the part of the system to endorse and pursue an agenda for raising standards and closing the gap.

2. Commitment to changing context at all levels involves the realization by leaders at all levels that they are changing the culture of schools and districts.

3. Lateral capacity-building through networks means identifying and investing in strategies that promote schools learning from each other.

4. Intelligent accountability and vertical relationships focus on developing great self-review capacity in the context of transparent external accountability.

5. Deep learning means that the system is continually pushing the envelope to address the fundamental learning goals of thinking and problem-solving skills, teamwork, and learning across the curriculum.

6. Dual commitment to short-term and long-term results requires system leaders to realize that they must pursue simultaneously short-term increases in student achievement and mid- to long-term results. They must lay the foundation for the long-term learning of all students.

7. Cyclical energizing emphasizes that "achievement at all costs" is self-defeating. Capacity must be built over time. Periods of intense development must be coupled with opportunities to recoup. Sustainability is about energy more than it is about time. Thus, monitoring and stimulating energy are key.

8. The long lever of leadership—leaders fostering the development of other leaders by widening their sphere of commitment and participation—is an integral part of this agenda. In this sense, the main mark of a school principal at the end of his or her tenure is not just his or her impact on the bottom line of student achievement, but equally on how many good leaders he or she leaves behind who can go even further. This is the long lever of

leadership. Leaders also need to help provide wider learning experiences through networks, clusters, paired schools, and other lateral capacity-building strategies.

Learning from each other. The third point in moving this ambitious agenda forward is the critical importance of learning from each other. We know this but need to address it explicitly with respect to tri-level reform. School cultures improve when teachers within the school learn from each other on an ongoing basis. District cultures improve when schools learn from each other, and when districts learn from one another. When schools or districts want to know where to start reform, they would be wise to conduct site visits to other schools or districts that are further down the road.

During a site visit, teams from the visiting school or district prepare questions for the host school and then gather data to address these questions. They then examine their findings and identify specific actions to take. This is an example of continuous learning that includes seeking out better information and learning from one's own experiences and from the experiences of others.

In addition, states engaged in tri-level reform need to learn from each other (both within and across countries). The learning principles are no different, just applied on a larger scale. Paying attention to the growing knowledge base, problem solving and learning through reflection, cultivating networks of interaction, and enlarging the world view are all part and parcel of increasing capacity and changing.

The danger of waiting for others to act. Finally, it would be a fundamental misunderstanding of systems theory to assume that the system should change first. Each of us *is* the system; there is no chicken and egg. We must connect with others to change whatever parts of the system we can. Whenever one is acting to promote professional learning communities, there should be an obligation to connect it to larger issues—bigger dots, if you will. Waiting for others to act virtually guarantees preservation of the status quo. If individuals are proactive, they stimulate others and make it more likely that the system will begin to change, resulting in new breakthroughs.

Engaging the Three Levels for System-Wide Success

The purpose of this entire agenda is twofold (Fullan, 2003): (1) to constantly seek and refine better ideas and practices (the knowledge dimension) and (2) to foster greater cohesion and shared commitment toward a higher purpose (the moral imperative). When all three levels—school/community, district or regional, and state or province—are engaged in this agenda, it will be possible to make substantial progress. Huge accomplishments literally become more within our reach. But they can only become doable if we make them system-wide pursuits. In the absence of tri-level participation, professional learning communities on any scale will be impossible to achieve. Professional learning communities writ large is everyone's agenda across the tri-levels.

References

DuFour, R. (2004). What is a "professional learning community"? *Educational Leadership, 61*(8), 6–11.

Fullan, M. (2003). *The moral imperative of school leadership.* Thousand Oaks, CA: Corwin Press; Toronto: Ontario Principals' Council.

Fullan, M. (2005a). *Leadership and sustainability.* Thousand Oaks, CA: Corwin Press; Toronto: Ontario Principals' Council.

Fullan, M. (2005b). *System thinkers in action: Beyond the plateau.* London: Department for Education and Skills. Pamphlet prepared for the Innovation Unit.

Fullan, M., Bertani, A., & Quinn, J. (2004). Lessons from district-wide reform. *Educational Leadership, 61*(6), 42–46.

Hargreaves, A., & Fink, D. (in press). *Sustainable leadership.* San Francisco: Jossey-Bass.

Newmann, F., King, B., & Youngs, P. (2000, April). *Professional development that addresses school capacity.* Paper presented at the annual meeting of the American Educational Research Association, New Orleans, LA.

Chapter 12

Closing the Knowing-Doing Gap

Richard DuFour, Robert Eaker, and Rebecca DuFour

We often pose this question to groups with whom we work: "If we could present an absolutely irrefutable case that the successful implementation of professional learning community concepts in your school will result in higher levels of student achievement and greater professional satisfaction for your educators, would you be willing to make substantive changes in your traditional practices to effect that successful implementation?"

We are confident we can make a compelling case for PLCs. For those who would be persuaded by a clear consensus of the leading thinkers in the field, we point to the authors of this book and many other renowned educational leaders who endorse the concept. For those who want a solid research base in support of PLCs, we can provide it. For those who are skeptical of research and want to see actual examples of schools and hear from the practitioners who have created PLCs, we can refer them to schools at all levels.

In fact, it is not difficult to build a strong case for the concepts upon which the PLC model is based, and for years we looked for just the right argument—the most persuasive metaphor, the best powerful illustrative example, the clinching closing argument—that would be so compelling that educators *en masse* would acknowledge that the PLC model was preferable to their traditional practices.

But, at some point, a growing realization began to seep into our work. Gradually it became clear that educators *knew* PLC practices were preferable to what they had been doing. They were reasonably familiar with the practices of high-performing schools, and if they did not have that knowledge, it was readily available to them in scores of books that were easily accessible. And yet they did not *act* on that knowledge. This discrepancy between knowing and doing did not simply apply to whole school reform; it also applied to practices *within* the school. Educators often recognized that there were persistent and significant differences in student achievement within classrooms in the same school, but they did nothing to come to a deep understanding regarding those differences in ways that might impact teacher pedagogy. Jeffrey Pfeffer and Robert Sutton (2000) describe this phenomenon of the disconnect between knowledge and action as one of the "great mysteries in organizational management: why knowledge of what needs to be done frequently fails to result in action or behavior consistent with that knowledge" (p. 4).

Turning Knowledge Into Action

In compiling the chapters of this book, it was our hope to give educators access to the best thinking of our most influential educational leaders and the best practices that are currently in place in North America's most effective schools. It was our intent to help educators build shared knowledge about the steps they must take to make progress toward the goal of high levels of learning for all students. But we recognize that unless those educators *act* on that knowledge, there is no reason to expect better results in their schools.

As Larry Lezotte mentioned in his chapter, Ron Edmonds would often remind the teachers and administrators with whom he worked that educators already knew more than they needed to know to improve their schools. Yet today, more than 30 years later, many of the same ineffective practices are still in place. Knowing what needs to be done is necessary, but it is not sufficient. Therefore, we have decided to conclude this book with both a review of the causes of the knowing-doing gap and with a presentation of specific strategies for addressing each cause. In doing so, we rely heavily on the work of Pfeffer and Sutton who have done extensive research into the issue. Although their research dealt exclusively with the private sector, their findings hold powerful lessons for educators who attempt to apply the PLC concept and strategies in their schools; for ultimately, teachers and administrators will face the challenge of turning knowledge about how to enhance school performance into actions consistent with that knowledge.

Ten Barriers to Action and How to Overcome Them

1. Substituting a decision for action. Many school systems suffer from the delusion that a decision made by someone higher in the organization will actually cause people throughout the organization to act in new ways. A classic example of this phenomenon at work is the way in which state standards and district curriculum guides have been passed down to teachers with an assumption that teachers would actually use those documents as instruments for changing the content of their instruction. In fact, Marzano (2003) found an enormous discrepancy between the "intended curriculum" designed by state boards of education and district curriculum coordinators and the "implemented curriculum" that is actually taught by teachers when they closed their classroom doors.

Educators who promote an action orientation avoid this trap by closely monitoring the *implementation* of decisions. They create follow-up processes that ensure decisions result in action. For example, a principal who was determined to close the knowing-doing gap between the intended curriculum and the implemented curriculum would work with staff to ensure that a team of teachers responsible for the same course or grade level would:

- Build shared knowledge about the most essential learning by collaboratively studying state standards, district curriculum guides, state and district assessment instruments, student performance on past assessments, the recommendations of the teachers in the next grade level or course, and so on.

- Identify and commit to teach the most essential outcomes or "power standards" as Doug Reeves suggests.

- Develop a plan to ensure common pacing of the curriculum.

- Create frequent formative assessments to monitor each student's learning.

- Establish a common standard to determine proficiency and establish agreed-upon criteria to be used in assessing the quality of student work.

- Analyze the results from each formative assessment and develop a plan to address areas of concern both for students in general as well as for individual students.

Furthermore, the principal would do more than simply work with staff to create this process and hope for the best. He or she would monitor the implementation of each step by asking teams to submit specific products associated with each step. Educators who hope to close the knowing-doing gap will acknowledge the truth of Pfeffer and Sutton's (2000) admonition that "a decision, by itself, changes nothing" (p. 33), and therefore they will create systems and processes to monitor the implementation of decisions.

2. Substituting mission for action. Many schools spend months developing profound and lofty mission statements and then believe that all staff will automatically begin to act in ways that are consistent with the mission. We have seen little evidence to suggest a strong correlation between a written mission statement and educators whose actions demonstrate that they share a strong sense of common purpose.

The true mission of a school is revealed by what people do, not by what they say. Therefore, educators committed to bringing their mission statements to life in their school are relentless in examining every practice, procedure, and decision and in asking, "Is this consistent with our mission of high levels of learning for all students?"

In schools that progress as PLCs, staff members quickly move beyond mission statements to clarify the characteristics of the school they are trying to create in order to achieve their mission. They develop a shared vision of the school that is clear and compelling. Just as importantly, they identify the collective commitments each staff member must demonstrate if the school is to move toward its vision. These commitments are stated not as beliefs, but as specific behaviors or actions that clarify how individual staff members can contribute to the successful implementation of the vision. Finally, the staff identifies specific goals or indicators that serve as benchmarks of their progress—targets and timelines that demand action if they are to be achieved. In *Professional Learning Communities at Work* (1998), we described this attention to clarifying mission, vision, collective commitments, and goals as building the foundation of a PLC. Every step in the process is designed to close the knowing-doing gap. Educators who hope to build PLCs will focus less on writing mission statements and more on demonstrating their missions at work through their day-to-day actions.

3. Planning as a substitute for action. Pfeffer and Sutton (2000) concluded that "existing research on the effectiveness of formal planning is clear: Planning is essentially unrelated to organizational performance" (p. 42). They could find no evidence to suggest that how much effort an organization devoted to planning or even how well it did in planning impacted how well it performed.

Nevertheless, many school districts continue to substitute elaborate strategic planning processes for doing the actual work of school improvement. Mike Schmoker (2004) offers a scathing indictment of this tendency for school districts to focus on strategic planning rather than action. He cites the tendency to commit to "far more activities and initiatives than anyone could possibly monitor, much less successfully implement" (p. 426). Douglas Reeves (2002) concurs, wryly observing that "all the plans I have examined have one thing in common: they are very, very large" (p. 104). Schmoker also criticizes the confusion created by the lack of precision in the terminology of strategic planning. Terms such as "goals," "action steps," and "results" are often used interchangeably, creating the impression that merely engaging in an activity is evidence of achieving a goal. He alleges that initiatives are often adopted to fulfill a personal or political agenda or to embrace the fad *du jour* rather than on the basis of their impact on student achievement. He blasts the underlying assumption of strategic planning: "The most vital, high leverage thinking is done primarily by 'planners' before the school year begins, rather than by teaching practitioners *throughout* the year." Finally, he laments the fact that "instructional quality—and levels of achievement—were typically unaffected" by strategic planning processes (pp. 426–427).

Schmoker does more than criticize the annual strategic planning process: he offers an alternative. He calls for teaching teams to work together in true learning communities committed to "continuous, collective, short-term experimentation, judgment, and adjustment" (p. 427). He envisions a team of teachers working collaboratively to agree on essential learning, develop frequent, short-term common assessments, analyze the results, and make adjustments to their instruction—not annually, but as part of a continuous cycle of improvement. He is convinced that the short-term wins teachers will experience as a result of this process can provide the momentum necessary to sustain the school improvement process. In brief, he calls upon teachers to *act* in partnership with their colleagues, and he insists that their actions will lead to deeper levels of understanding, commitment, and effectiveness than any strategic plan. Finally, he calls upon district offices to abandon complex strategic planning in favor of ensuring that this continuous cycle of improvement be established in every school.

4. Complexity as a barrier to action. An offshoot of the strategic planning problem is the issue of unnecessary complexity. Pfeffer and Sutton (2000) found that the organizations that were better at learning and translating knowledge into action limited their goals and initiatives and "understood the virtue of simple language, simple structures, simple concepts, and the power of common sense" (p. 59). Schools often fail to demonstrate that understanding. Education has taken on its own jargon and acronym-filled vocabulary that often serves to obscure issues rather than clarify them. Strategic plans are presented in volumes. Teachers are buried in data. Federal, state, and district improvement initiatives wash upon schools in constant waves. It is easy for educators to fall victim to the malady of paralysis by analysis.

Jim Collins (2001) determined that great organizations were able to avoid this affliction by simplifying "a complex world into a single organizing idea, a basic principle, or concept that unifies and guides everything" (p. 91). Tichy (1997) found the same thing, observing that the leaders of effective organizations were able to articulate a "big idea" that provided direction and became a frame of reference for all decisions.

Those who hope to lead the process of building a PLC will return, with boorish redundancy, to the big ideas that drive the concept. Their message will be simple:

> The purpose of our school is to see to it that all our students learn at high levels, and the future of our students depends on our success. We must

work collaboratively to achieve that purpose, because it is impossible to accomplish if we work in isolation. And we must continually assess our effectiveness in achieving our purpose on the basis of results—tangible evidence that our students are acquiring the knowledge, skills, and dispositions we feel are essential to their future success.

This message would not be reserved for faculty meetings at the beginning of the school year, but would become a mantra articulated in words and deeds at every opportunity. More importantly, it would become the frame of reference for decisions on a day-to-day basis. When a staff comes to embrace this big idea, and is willing to honestly assess the current reality in the school, they are prompted to act, and the decisions about what to do and what to stop doing become self-evident (Collins, 2001).

A second strategy for addressing this barrier to action is to translate the change process into a series of manageable tasks. Creating a PLC is indeed a complex endeavor. Furthermore, it is a task that is never quite complete, a journey with no final destination. Schools never "arrive" as a PLC—they simply drive the concept deeper and deeper into their culture. We have seen faculties become daunted by the challenge once the realization sinks in that this is an ongoing process rather than a new program to be adopted or a project to complete. But as the Chinese proverb advises, "the journey of a thousand miles begins with a single step." At the same time leaders of the process are championing the big ideas of a PLC, they must break down the school's journey into a series of small, incremental steps that goad people to action.

For example, in attempting to build the capacity of a staff to function in high-performing teams, a principal could work with the staff to create specific targets and timelines for the completion of a series of tasks that call upon the team to create products to guide their work. It could be as simple as the following calendar for team products:

By the end of the . . .

- **second week** of school, each team will present the team norms and protocols that will guide the interactions and work of the team.

- **fourth week** of school, each team will present its SMART goal.

- **sixth week** of school, each team will present a listing of the essential learning or power standards all students are to achieve in the first semester.

- **eighth week** of school, each team will present a common formative assessment it is using to assess each student's mastery of essential learning.

- **tenth week** of school, each team will present its analysis of student performance on the common assessment, including areas of strengths and weaknesses and strategies for addressing those students who are experiencing difficulty.

5. Mindless precedent as a barrier to action. Anyone who has proposed an initiative to a faculty for improving a school has heard such responses as, "But that's not the way we have always done it," "Are you saying we have been doing it wrong all this time?" and "The way we have done it has always worked fine for us; if it ain't broke, don't fix it." Pfeffer and Sutton (2000) refer to this way of thinking as "mindless precedent." The culture of any organization is found in the assumptions, beliefs, expectations, and habits that constitute the norm for its people, but these elements of culture tend to go unexamined. Organizations can become trapped by their culture and the implicit theories of behavior or unexamined assumptions that guide their decisions and actions. Therefore, challenges to culture are likely to result in appeals to precedent as a reason for not doing differently.

The single best strategy for addressing this barrier to action is to bring the unstated assumptions that created the precedent to the surface—to challenge people to think carefully about the assumptions underlying their practice. Senge et al. (2000) refer to this practice as "climbing the ladder of inference," and contend that people routinely take each step unconsciously. They begin by gathering observable data, selecting the data that fit their assumptions, using their personal experience to add meaning to the data, making assumptions, drawing conclusions, adopting beliefs, and finally, acting on the data. The request that someone act in new ways is made when the person is at the end of this process rather than the beginning and is likely to result in opposition.

Leaders who hope to help staff climb the ladder of inference would engage in the process of "advocacy and inquiry" (Senge et al., 2000). Instead of merely proposing new action, they would attempt to build shared knowledge among the staff and share the assumptions that led to the proposal. They would then encourage staff to bring their assumptions to the forefront and engage in honest dialogue about similarities and differences.

For example, an elementary school principal might make a statement such as the one in the feature box beginning on page 237 while proposing that teachers build common, team-based formative assessments to be administered periodically rather than relying solely on each teacher to create his or her own assessments.

When leaders build shared knowledge of best practice and give everyone on the staff access to the same information, they increase the likelihood that the staff will arrive at the same conclusions regarding the benefits of acting in new ways. When they present the assumptions that lead to their proposal, encourage staff to examine those assumptions, and invite them to articulate the assumptions behind their current practice, they can help a staff free itself from mindless precedent as a barrier to action.

6. Internal competition as a barrier to action. Pfeffer and Sutton (2000) found that when the culture of an organization was characterized by internal competition, when people refused to acknowledge that they might learn from their colleagues, they were less likely to reduce the knowing-doing gap. They viewed such a culture as particularly toxic because "interdependence is what organizations are about. . . . The willingness of individuals to cooperate with other members of the organization is one of the major determinants of organizational effectiveness and efficiency." People can learn from one another, build shared knowledge, and develop and transfer skill and wisdom only in a "sharing culture . . . a climate in which people talk and interact comfortably, in part, because they are not competing against each other" (p. 197).

Sample Proposal and Assumptions

Let me state the assumptions that have led me to this proposal for common assessments. First, I have provided you with the research on effective schools and effective teaching, both of which cite the importance of frequent monitoring of student learning. I assume frequent and timely monitoring of student learning is essential to effective teaching, and I assume that good teachers are monitoring student learning in a variety of ways, all the time.

Second, when teachers work together to build common assessments that they administer to their students several times during the year, I assume they benefit in the following ways:

It is more efficient and will save time for teachers. Instead of each teacher being responsible for creating every assessment for every essential skill, a team of teachers can divide the work and each contribute just a portion of the common assessment. For example, one teacher could focus on assessing the ability of students to distinguish between the main idea and details while another focuses on student understanding of cause and effect.

It will help us to promote and monitor common academic goals and consistent pacing in our curriculum. Teachers will continue to have considerable autonomy. They will be free to use whatever instructional strategies they find most effective, and they can pace day-to-day instruction according to their best judgment—with two provisions. First, all students will have access to the same essential learning, regardless of who their teacher might be. Second, a teacher must ensure students are prepared for the periodic common team assessment of that essential learning.

It will provide teachers with information rather than data. Teachers have never lacked for data. Every time a teacher gives a test, he or she can establish mean, mode, median, standard deviation, percentage proficient, and so on. But unless teachers have a basis of comparison,

(continued)

Sample Proposal and Assumptions (continued)

data will not inform their practice by helping them to understand the strengths and weaknesses of their instruction. Data can serve as a catalyst for improvement only when teachers have a basis of comparison: How well do my students understand this concept compared to other, similar students in our school who are attempting to master the same concept? Common assessments provide teachers with that information and thus are superior to assessments prepared by individual teachers.

It will help all students learn. When individual teachers have this kind of powerful information and the support of their teammates, they can build on their strengths and address their weaknesses and become more and more effective in helping all students learn.

It will help create a collective response to assist students. When a team has access to this information regarding the achievement of all the students entrusted to them, they can identify and address concerns in their program and create a collective response to assist students who are experiencing difficulty.

I recognize that you may have concerns regarding the time it will take to develop these common assessments. I am convinced, however, that we can generate ways to provide you with that time during your regular contractual day. I also understand that some of you may look upon this as another layer of assessment that will result in less time for instruction. My assumption is that these common assessments will simply replace some of the individual tests you have been using, and that you will not lose time for instruction because of them.

So these are the assumptions that led me to conclude that common grade-level assessments could be a powerful tool in our effort to help all students achieve at high levels. I'm very interested in your response to my assumptions. Are there any of them you would question? And I am also very interested in hearing the assumptions that would lead us to conclude that it is more beneficial to students and teachers to rely solely on assessments created by the individual teacher.

What steps can leaders take to overcome this barrier and create a "sharing culture"? Leaders must start by shifting their focus from evaluating and supervising individuals to developing the capacity of both teams and the entire school to work collaboratively. Pfeffer and Sutton contend that an emphasis on the evaluation of individuals fostered internal competition and discouraged interdependent behaviors such as knowledge sharing, collaboration, and mutual assistance. Unfortunately, most teacher evaluation programs are based on the premise that performance comes from the sum of individual actions rather than the ability to work interdependently. Rick DuFour (2002) has described his conversion from the peripatetic principal (who attempted to prove he was the instructional leader by devoting hours to observing individual teachers in their classrooms) to a learning leader who shifted his energies to develop the capacity of collaborative teacher teams whose members could learn from one another rather than from the principal. Teachers in his school soon came to realize that their evaluation was far more dependent upon their ongoing participation in and contribution to their collaborative team than their classroom practices on that rare day when the principal dropped in to observe.

Another step to diminish internal competition is to examine the explicit and implicit reward system in the school. The principal or the Parent/Teacher Association that presents the annual "Teacher of the Year" award may have the best of intentions, but it is exactly the wrong thing to do. It ensures one winner and establishes everyone else as a loser. We have known for over a quarter century that the most effective organizations purposefully design their reward systems to ensure a lot of winners and to celebrate those winners at every opportunity

(Peters & Waterman, 1982). When teams become the focus of celebration and every team feels it too has the opportunity to be recognized and applauded, schools begin to move away from a culture of internal competition and toward a sharing culture.

The third and most powerful strategy for reducing internal competition is to ensure that every collaborative team has identified and is pursuing a common goal that can only be achieved through interdependent action. In fact, our very definition of a team is a group of people working together *interdependently* to achieve *common goals* (DuFour, DuFour, Eaker, & Karhanek, 2004). If a goal can be achieved without contributions from each member of the group, then the school has not fostered collaboration. And if a group of teachers meets on a regular basis, but they have no specific goal they are trying to achieve, then they are not a collaborative team. Both interdependence and a common goal are essential to developing collaborative teams and a culture of sharing.

The term "goal" has been used so loosely in education that most teams will need some assistance in defining their goal. The SMART goal acronym (Conzemius & O'Neill, 2002) can be very helpful in this process. Leaders should help teams develop goals that are:

> **Strategic and Specific:** The team goal is aligned with a broader school or district goal and the language is precise rather than vague.

> **Measurable:** The team has a clear idea of the measures it will use to assess its progress toward the goal.

Attainable: The goal is ambitious enough to demand that team members act in new ways in their classrooms, but not so ambitious that it discourages effort.

Results-Oriented: The goal focuses on the intended results (evidence of student learning) rather than on teacher activities such as the creation of new materials.

Timebound: The team has established a timeline for the achievement of the goal.

Leaders who hope to overcome the barrier of internal competition and foster a collaborative culture will put staff in the position where they must work interdependently to achieve a common goal. By doing so, they are stimulating staff to act in new ways.

7. Badly designed measurement systems as a barrier to action. Pfeffer and Sutton found that badly-designed and unnecessarily complex measurement processes are among the biggest barriers to turning knowledge into action. These ineffective systems typically focus on end-of-process measures—measures that tell how well we have done—rather than in-process measures that help people understand what is going right and what is going wrong. The end-of-process measures are "too far removed from the process in many instances to guide behavior and permit knowledge to be developed and turned into action" (p. 154). This tendency to measure people on outcomes without giving them in-process measurement creates stress and frustration, but does little to improve results.

Clearly, Pfeffer and Sutton are drawing a distinction between "formative" (that is, in-process) assessments that give people timely and useful information about how they need to act and "summative" (that is, end-of-process) assessments that are of little use in guiding behavior. It is the contrast Douglas Reeves refers to in his chapter when he states that formative assessments are to summative assessments as physical examinations are to autopsies. Teachers who find out over the summer that their students from the previous year did not do well on the state exam have not been provided with the timely information they need to help all their students acquire the essential knowledge and skills.

It should be evident to even the most casual reader of this book that the respective authors have consistently stressed the power of formative assessments to improve teaching, help more students learn at higher levels, and foster a collaborative culture. We cannot imagine any school succeeding in its effort to create a professional learning community without a commitment to formative assessments—assessments used for learning.

Another of the measurement system problems uncovered by Pfeffer and Sutton was the tendency to measure far too many things. Many organizations have taken the adage of "what gets measured gets done" to mean that if we measure more, then more will get done. Action-oriented organizations do not, however, have a plethora of outcomes measures. They measure things most essential to their culture and present those measurements to employees in clear, easily understandable terms that then guide the work.

Again, the parallels with education are readily apparent. In too many schools, teachers are buried in measurement data that focus on too many outcomes and are presented in unnecessarily complex ways. Douglas Reeves (2002) advises that the cardinal principle of quality measurement states "it is more important to measure a few things frequently than to measure a lot of things infrequently" (p. 12). Therefore, leaders who hope to build PLCs will help staff:

- Narrow their focus to measurements of the most essential outcomes.

- Create formative assessment systems that give teachers frequent and timely feedback on the learning of their students.

- Ensure that the information from such assessments is easily accessible to teachers and presented in a clear and straightforward way. When teachers begin openly sharing such data with each other and using it to improve their practice, the school is making tremendous progress on its PLC journey.

8. An external focus as a barrier to action. Another barrier to an action orientation is an external focus—looking at the conditions outside of the organization that impede its progress or success. This tendency is widespread because people who are determined not to act can always find a reason to justify inaction. The problem is pervasive in education. In his chapter, Dennis Sparks cites a tradition of educator "dependence on those outside the school for solutions to problems" as one of the major barriers to becoming a PLC.

In an article Rick DuFour wrote for the *Journal of Staff Development* (2004), he recounted meeting with a high school faculty that wanted his ideas for acquiring more resources. He admitted he did not have much to offer in terms of getting more resources in the cash-starved district, but asked the staff to list their ideas for improving student achievement in the school. In 5 minutes they came up with the following list:

- More financial support from the state
- Smaller class sizes
- More support staff to assist students and teachers
- Fewer preparations for teachers
- More supportive parents
- Abolition of state testing
- Higher teacher salaries to reflect the importance of the profession
- More planning time for teachers
- Fewer initiatives from the central office
- Better preparation of students in the middle school
- Better facilities
- More access to technology for students and staff
- Students with a stronger work ethic and reduced sense of entitlement
- More current textbooks and instructional materials
- More financial support for attendance at conferences and workshops

Rick agreed that he could endorse most of the items on the list as things that could benefit them and the school, but he asked if they would consider another list, which included:

- Academic goals for every student that are so clear, focused, and widely understood that students taking the same course from different teachers are ensured the opportunity to learn the same essential curriculum

- Close monitoring of each student's learning on a frequent and timely basis through the use of formative assessments that identify problems both for students in general as well as for individual students

- A systematic plan to give extra time and support to students experiencing initial difficulty in learning

- Strong parent partnerships with the school based on frequent two-way communication regarding the progress of each student in each course

- Meaningful and timely information to every teacher clarifying how well his or her students have met learning goals compared with the students of colleagues

- A collaborative culture in which teachers work together in teams to analyze student achievement on common assessments, develop strategies to improve levels of achievement, and help each other build on their strengths and address their weaknesses

- A general assumption that it is the school's job to see to it that all students learn rather than merely be taught, and the expectation that all students can and should learn at high levels

- A safe and orderly environment with clear parameters for student behavior, consistent enforcement of those parameters, and an overarching stipulation that members of the school community treat each other with mutual respect

When he asked the staff to compare and contrast the two lists, the staff ultimately acknowledged that the first list required someone else to take action to improve the school, while they could initiate the actions on the second list. They also grudgingly acknowledged that, in general, they had not yet taken those actions.

Of course another difference between the two lists warrants particular emphasis. The items on the second list have a much more powerful impact on student achievement than those on the first. Educators who honestly confront these facts will face conflicting emotions. On the one hand, it is reasonable and right for educators to convey to the public a sense of urgency regarding the situations they confront and the pressing need for more resources to meet the enormous challenges they face. On the other hand, they must also acknowledge that there is much they can and should do that lies within their sphere of influence to improve teaching and learning in their schools.

So leaders who hope to foster an action orientation will reframe the conversation from things that cannot be done and the problems the school cannot control to a discussion of the specific steps the school can and must take, right now, to overcome barriers and help more students to achieve at higher levels. A focus outward—identifying the steps someone else must take to improve the situation—is counterproductive. Educators create a results orientation in their schools when they stop looking out the window for solutions to their problems and start looking in the mirror.

9. A focus on attitudes as a barrier to action. Perhaps the most frequent rationale we hear when pressing educators to begin taking action toward building a PLC is their contention that some of their colleagues are not "ready" to act. They have not been persuaded, or all of their concerns have not been resolved, or they are simply resistant to change. Their premise, stated in many different forms, is that they cannot go forward until all staff members have a positive attitude toward the proposed action.

This premise must be re-examined. A faculty that contends that every staff member must endorse a change initiative before that change can be implemented is a school that is forever doomed to suffer from the knowing-doing gap. Any complex organization that gives every member of the group veto power over implementing new ideas will be paralyzed in the status quo. In our work with schools we have offered a different benchmark for action: "We will move forward when all points of view have been heard and considered, and the will of the group becomes evident—even to those who most oppose it."

This benchmark acknowledges that some people will not commit to a course of action until they have had some experience in taking that action. As Pfeffer and Sutton contend, "There is a large literature demonstrating that attitudes *follow* behavior. That means people accept new beliefs as a result of changing their behavior . . . action can influence talk even more powerfully than talk can influence actions" (p. 65).

So rather than devoting weeks and months to dialogue in an attempt to persuade staff about the merits of acting in new ways, leaders of the PLC initiative will attempt to build shared knowledge regarding the initiative until a critical mass is ready to support moving forward. They will then create conditions that require people to behave in new ways in the hope that these new experiences will affect attitudes and beliefs in a positive way.

It is important, however, that leaders do more than prompt a staff to take new actions: they must consistently communicate the underlying rationale to support the action. There is ample evidence that educators who merely mimic the successful practices of another school are unlikely to replicate that success. For example, providing teachers with unstructured time to collaborate in the wrong school culture will only reinforce the negative aspects of the culture. Eventually a staff must come to understand the underlying assumptions and collective commitments that constitute the foundation of the practices. As Pfeffer and Sutton advise, leaders must focus not only on *how*—the detailed practices and procedures they are promoting—but also on *why*—the assumptions that underlie the procedures.

School leaders who are committed to developing the capacity of a staff to function as a PLC will wage the battle on two fronts. It is imperative that they create conditions that result in people acting in new ways, but it is equally imperative that they provide coherence to those actions with consistent messages about the big ideas that give meaning to the actions.

10. Training as a substitute for action. Pfeffer and Sutton summarized their research with a single, powerful sentence: "The solution to the knowing-doing gap is deceptively simple; embed more of the process of acquiring new knowledge in the actual doing of the task and less in formal training programs that are frequently less effective" (p. 27). They found that the knowledge gained by doing was far more likely to be implemented than knowledge acquired from reading, listening, or even thinking. Educational researchers have come to the same conclusion. There is now general agreement that the most powerful staff development is job-embedded—teachers learning together as part of their routine work practice.

We have seen schools and districts use traditional staff development as a strategy to procrastinate. Well-intentioned administrators believe that their teachers must receive formal training in a host of new skills *before* they can start doing the work of a PLC. They create ambitious, long-term training programs designed to help teachers interpret state standards, clarify power standards, write effective assessments, analyze data, reach consensus, resolve conflict, develop goals, and so on. The main effect of this approach is to ensure that teachers will be subject to years of training before they are called upon to do the work of creating a PLC. Teachers may indeed need training in these areas, but that training should be provided "just in time"—as they are doing the work—rather than in preparation to do the work.

We often work with schools over a number of days to provide them with the conceptual framework of a PLC, to identify specific strategies for implementing the concept, to answer their questions, and to help them develop plans for moving forward. At the end of our time together, they often ask if they can make arrangements for "advanced" PLC training. In fact, advanced PLC training does not come from formal training: it comes from doing the work of PLCs. It comes from trying a lot of things, learning from what works and what does not, thinking about what was learned, making adjustments, and trying again. As Pfeffer and Sutton concluded, "Knowing by doing develops a deeper and more profound level of understanding and eliminates the knowing-doing gap" (p. 251).

Educators instinctively know this to be true. Most of us spent 4 or 5 years preparing to be teachers. We took courses in content and methodology. We observed classrooms as part of our undergraduate experience. We worked under the direction of a supervising teacher as a student teacher. Virtually all of us would agree, however, that we learned more about teaching in our first semester in the classroom than we did in all the years we spent preparing to be a teacher. The same is true of building a PLC. The school that actually *does* the work of a PLC will develop its capacity to help all students learn far more effectively than the school that spends years preparing to be a PLC.

When we wrote *Professional Learning Communities at Work* in 1998, we listed an "action orientation" as one of the characteristics of PLCs. In retrospect, we did not give nearly enough emphasis to that attribute. Until educators become relentlessly action oriented, they will do little to close the knowing-doing gap or to develop their capacity to function as a PLC.

Creating PLCs: Difficult, But Doable

This review of some of the barriers educators will face in their attempt to transform their schools into PLCs is not intended to discourage them from making the effort, but rather is offered to help them approach the task intelligently. Building a PLC is difficult, but it is also unquestionably *doable.* We use that word very purposefully. Educators will be required to act in new ways, to *do* differently. They will confront decisions regarding what needs to be done and what they need to stop doing, but as Collins (2001) emphasizes, *"You absolutely cannot make a series of good decisions without first confronting the brutal facts"* (p. 70). There are brutal facts regarding the traditional structure and culture of schools that must be brought to the surface, examined, and discussed in the process of building a PLC. Educators who acknowledge and honestly assess their current reality are far more likely to be successful in changing it.

It is also important for educators to approach the task with a sense of reality regarding the challenges they will face. As Seymour Sarason (1995) wrote:

> . . . the decision to undertake change more often than not is accompanied by a kind of optimism and rosy view of the future that, temporarily at least, obscures the predictable turmoil ahead. But that turmoil cannot be avoided and how well it is coped with separates the boys from the men, the girls from the women. It is . . . rough stuff . . . it has no end point, it is a continuous process, there are breakthroughs but also brick walls. *And it is indisputably worthwhile.* (p. vii, italics added)

We know of no faculties that have developed their capacity to create a PLC that did not experience failure and conflict along the way. Failure and conflict are inevitable byproducts of substantive change processes. Those who assume they can completely avoid these problems are either naïve or arrogant. The challenge is not avoidance; the challenge is working through the conflict and viewing an attempt gone awry as a chance to begin again more intelligently.

But while the process of building a PLC presents significant challenges, the faculties who have been successful in doing so inevitably concur with Sarason's assertion that it was "indisputably worthwhile." They report a greater sense of accomplishment and self-efficacy. They describe the connection and comradeship they have developed with colleagues. They advise that their job is more satisfying and more manageable, and that they feel a stronger sense of professionalism. And they revel in the knowledge that they are becoming more effective in making a positive difference in the lives of their students.

We sincerely believe that public education stands at an important crossroads. At no time in our history have we, as a profession, possessed a clearer sense of what it takes to help all students learn at high levels. The question remains: Will we demonstrate the discipline and tenacity to act on that knowledge? Will the professional learning community concept truly become an idea whose time has come—an idea that transforms schooling? Or will its promise and potential be lost?

The words of Martin Luther King, Jr., (1967) challenged another generation to no longer delay in making a profoundly moral choice. Those words present a fitting challenge to contemporary educators as they are called upon to seize this opportunity to do the right thing for their students and themselves.

> We are now faced with the fact that tomorrow is today. We are confronted with the fierce urgency of now. In this unfolding conundrum of life and history there is such a thing as being too late. Procrastination is still the thief of time. . . . We must move past indecision to action. . . . Now let us begin. Now let us rededicate ourselves to the long and bitter—but beautiful—struggle for a new world. . . . The choice is ours, and though we might prefer it otherwise, we must choose in this crucial moment of human history.

It is our fervent hope that educators throughout North America will recognize the impact of their work upon the future lives of their students and make the crucial choice to transform their schools into professional learning communities.

References

Collins, J. (2001). *Good to great: Why some companies make the leap . . . and others don't.* New York: Harper Business.

Conzemius, A., & O'Neill, J. (2002). *The handbook for SMART school teams.* Bloomington, IN: Solution Tree (formerly National Educational Service).

DuFour, R. (2002). The learning-centered principal. *Educational Leadership, 59*(8), 12–15.

DuFour, R. (2004). Are you looking out the window or in a mirror? *Journal of Staff Development, 25*(3), 63–64.

DuFour, R., DuFour, R., Eaker, R., & Karhanek, G. (2004). *Whatever it takes: How professional learning communities respond when kids don't learn.* Bloomington, IN: Solution Tree (formerly National Educational Service).

DuFour, R., & Eaker, R. (1998). *Professional learning communities at work: Best practices for enhancing student achievement.* Bloomington, IN: Solution Tree (formerly National Educational Service).

King, M. L., Jr. (1967, April 4). *Beyond Vietnam.* Speech presented at Riverside Church in New York. Retrieved January 11, 2005, from http://www.stanford.edu/group/King/publications/speeches/Beyond_Vietnam.pdf

Marzano, R. (2003). *What works in schools: Translating research into action.* Alexandria, VA: Association for Supervision and Curriculum Development.

Peters, T., & Waterman, R. (1982). *In search of excellence: Lessons from America's best-run companies.* New York: Harper & Row.

Pfeffer, J., & Sutton, R. (2000). *The knowing-doing gap: How smart companies turn knowledge into action.* Boston: Harvard Business Press.

Reeves, D. (2002). *The leader's guide to standards: A blueprint for educational equity and excellence.* San Francisco: Jossey-Bass.

Sarason, S. (1995). Foreword. In A. Lieberman (Ed.), *The work of restructuring schools: Building from the ground up* (pp. vii–viii). New York: Teachers College Press.

Schmoker, M. (2004). Tipping point: From feckless reform to substantive instructional improvement. *Phi Delta Kappan, 85*(6), 424–432.

Senge, P., Cambron-McCabe, N., Lucas, T., Smith, B., Dutton, J., & Kleiner, A. (2000). *Schools that learn.* New York: Doubleday.

Tichy, N. (1997). *The leadership engine: How winning companies build leaders at every level.* New York: Harper Business.

Make the Most of Your
Professional Development Investment

Let Solution Tree schedule time for you and your staff with leading practitioners in the areas of:

- **Professional Learning Communities** with Richard DuFour, Robert Eaker, Rebecca DuFour, and associates
- **Effective Schools** with associates of Larry Lezotte
- **Assessment for Learning** with Rick Stiggins and associates
- **Crisis Management and Response** with Cheri Lovre
- **Discipline With Dignity** with Richard Curwin and Allen Mendler
- **SMART School Teams** with Jan O'Neill and Anne Conzemius
- **PASSport to Success** (parental involvement) with Vickie Burt
- **Peacemakers** (violence prevention) with Jeremy Shapiro

Additional presentations are available in the following areas:

- At-Risk Youth Issues
- Bullying Prevention/Teasing and Harassment
- Team Building and Collaborative Teams
- Data Collection and Analysis
- Embracing Diversity
- Literacy Development
- Motivating Techniques for Staff and Students

Solution Tree
formerly national educational service

304 W. Kirkwood Avenue
Bloomington, IN 47404-5132
(812) 336-7700
(800) 733-6786 (toll-free number)
FAX (812) 336-7790
e-mail: info@solution-tree.com
www.solution-tree.com

NEED MORE COPIES OR ADDITIONAL
RESOURCES ON THIS TOPIC?

Need more copies of this book? Want your own copy? Need additional resources on this topic? If so, you can order additional materials by using this form or by calling us toll free at (800) 733-6786 or (812) 336-7700. Or you can order by FAX at (812) 336-7790 or online at www.solution-tree.com.

Title	Price*	Qty	Total
On Common Ground: The Power of Professional Learning Communities	$ 29.95		
Whatever It Takes: How PLCs Respond When Kids Don't Learn	24.95		
Getting Started: Reculturing Schools to Become Professional Learning Communities	19.95		
Professional Learning Communities at Work (video set)	495.00		
Professional Learning Communities at Work (book)	24.95		
How to Develop a PLC: Passion and Persistence	24.95		
Through New Eyes: Examining the Culture of Your School	174.95		
Let's Talk About PLC: Getting Started	199.95		
The Handbook for SMART School Teams	54.95		
Professional Learning Communities at Work Online Course	349.00		
		SUBTOTAL	
		SHIPPING	
Continental U.S.: Please add 6% of order total. Outside continental U.S.: Please add 8% of order total.			
		HANDLING	
Continental U.S.: Please add $4. Outside continental U.S.: Please add $6.			
		TOTAL (U.S. funds)	

*Price subject to change without notice.

❑ Check enclosed   ❑ Purchase order enclosed
❑ Money order   ❑ VISA, MasterCard, Discover, or American Express (circle one)

Credit Card No._____ Exp. Date_____

Cardholder Signature _____

SHIP TO:

First Name_____ Last Name_____

Position _____

Institution Name_____

Address_____

City_____ State_____ ZIP_____

Phone_____ FAX_____

E-mail _____

Solution Tree
formerly national educational service

304 W. Kirkwood Avenue
Bloomington, IN 47404-5132
(812) 336-7700 • (800) 733-6786 (toll-free number)
FAX (812) 336-7790
e-mail: orders@solution-tree.com
www.solution-tree.com